EVERY MANAGER'S LEGAL GUIDE TO FIRING

INCLUDES EMPLOYEE TERMINATIONS AND WORK FORCE REDUCTIONS

EVERY MANAGER'S LEGAL GUIDE TO FIRING

INCLUDES EMPLOYEE TERMINATIONS AND WORK FORCE REDUCTIONS

August Bequai

BUSINESS ONE IRWIN
Homewood, IL 60430

Sponsoring editor: Susan Glinert Stevens, Ph.D.
Project editor: Jean Roberts
Production manager: Ann Cassady
Jacket design: Renée Klyczek Nordstrom
Compositor: TCSystems, Inc.
Typeface: 11/13 Century Schoolbook
Printer: The Book Press, Inc.

Library of Congress Cataloging-in-Publication Data

Bequai, August.
    Every manager's legal guide to firing: includes employee
terminations and work force reductions/by August Bequai.
        p.   cm.
    ISBN 1-55623-376-0
    1. Employees—Dismissal of—Law and legislation—United States—
Popular works.   2. Layoff systems—Law and legislation—United
States—Popular works.   3. Executives—United States—Handbooks.
manuals, etc.   I. Title.
KF3471.Z9B47   1991
344.73′012596—dc20
[347.30412596]   90–20509

Printed in the United States of America
1 2 3 4 5 6 7 8 9 0 BP 8 7 6 5 4 3 2 1

To the memory of Haxhi Bequai and Samuel Goldman, who both believed in ethics and professionalism

\

PREFACE

Are you afraid to fire a problem employee for fear that he or she will sue you? Well, your fears aren't groundless.

Termination has become a sort of lottery—and losing a firing case can be hard on your corporate pocketbook. The average jury verdict in wrongful discharge cases is $250,000; $450,000 awards to ex-employees aren't uncommon. Some experts predict that by the end of the 20th century, the average judgment could exceed $1 million. No wonder the number of termination cases is doubling every year.

Some of these cases are simply the result of living at a time when litigation has become the U.S. national game. Also, employees (particularly managers) are more savvy about their legal rights than were the workers of the past. And they're not shy about suing when they think they've been taken for a ride.

Employers seldom admit that they dig their own graves in termination cases, but they do. They beg for trouble when they don't treat employees the same, whether they're stock clerks or CEOs; when they don't have clear, standardized, well-disseminated policies and procedures for termination; when they don't follow their own rules; and when they don't keep scrupulous records of every firing and the events leading up to it.

Then, too, the economy ain't what it used to be. There was a time when managers didn't have to worry about the effect of mergers and buyouts on their work force; a time when businesses only occasionally went belly-up, when factories rarely shut down. Now the economic focus is on service rather than manufacturing industries. Foreign products have taken root in our consumer landscape. And spending cuts are sounding the death knell for many firms. As a result, more companies must think about large-scale layoffs and facility closings than ever before. Unfortunately, they don't always do things by the book . . . and they get sued by the employees they lay off.

Whether it involves a layoff or an outright firing, a termination lawsuit often begins with a discrimination complaint against an employer. A quarter of U.S. workers believe that their employers have discriminated against them because of their sex, race, religion, age, or disability, and at least half have taken legal action. You have probably seen some evidence of this: an African-American claiming that he or she has been fired because of racial discrimination, a female employee charging a male boss with sexual harassment or discriminatory treatment, an older worker alleging that he or she was let go because of age.

That's where *Every Manager's Legal Guide to Firing* comes in. It's designed to help managers who regularly deal with dismissal, discipline, and layoffs.

Every Manager's Legal Guide to Firing is different from other books on the subject that you may have come across. Many of the current volumes are how-to manuals aimed at human resources professionals, and they tend to emphasize the "touchy-feely" aspects of termination. Legalities rate a slim chapter, if they rate anything at all, because such books assume that their readers already know the legal ramifications of firing problem employees or laying off workers.

There are also books on termination law—usually ponderous tomes, written by lawyers for other lawyers. These books contain the right stuff, but they're full of obfuscating legal jargon and labyrinthine concepts. That's cold comfort to the desperate manager who's just been zapped with a government agency investigation or a lawsuit seeking millions in damages for a terminated employee.

Every Manager's Legal Guide to Firing presents time-tested ideas, programs, and procedures that even the most legally naive manager can implement to become "judgment-proof." The case studies, checklists, outlines, and illustrations should help managers:

1. Evaluate their current termination policies.
2. Assess the effectiveness of their personnel policies and procedures in fending off discrimination charges.

3. Take preventive action to reduce the possibility of being investigated by a government agency.
4. Identify and discipline problem employees without running the risk of litigation.
5. Deal with layoffs, plant closings, and mergers and acquisitions in a way that complies with the law.
6. Ensure that recordkeeping procedures are in line with federal, state, and local regulations.

Most of the theory (and there isn't much!) is in the first couple of chapters. Chapter 1, "The Firing Line," covers the at-will doctrine, the granddaddy of all hiring and firing law in the United States. In the old days, the at-will doctrine was all the legal ammunition you needed to fire an employee. Now, so many laws and court rulings have blunted its impact that your firing rights have been severely curtailed. Chapter 2 moves from the theory to the day-to-day realities of personnel law and explains how those realities affect you when you set out to discipline or fire your workers.

There are good reasons to fire an employee—reasons that stand up in court—and there are bad reasons, as you'll see in Chapter 3, "The Right Way to Fire." Chapter 4 takes an in-depth look at a very legitimate reason for termination: on-the-job drug and alcohol abuse. When should you test? What tests should you use? What about searching employees' lockers for drugs? Can you fire an employee for off-the-job substance abuse? These are just a few of the questions that "Poison in the Workplace" answers.

Employers have lost firing cases because they don't have a standard procedure for determining who should be fired for what, and how terminations should be handled. Chapter 5 gives you the lowdown on how to develop "Policies That Do the Job."

Inevitably, a terminated employee is going to sue you for wrongful discharge or discriminatory firing, even if you have the best policies in the universe. Chapter 6, "Lawyers, Employees, and Money," tells you what to expect from litigious employees and gives you an inside line on typical employee strategies. Chapter 7 offers tried-and-true defenses against employee lawsuits and hints on how to fight the good fight in "The Employer's Court."

Chapter 8 describes how to avoid "The Pink Slip Blues," which is what happens when lawsuits follow on the heels of mass layoffs or facility closings; it also warns about using layoffs as instruments for eliminating workers you can't get rid of any other way. Chapter 9 covers employment agreements, from full-blown employment contracts for independent contractors to special-purpose agreements for terminated employees. Chapter 10 emphasizes the importance of keeping clear and accurate records of every termination. And the final chapter speculates where firing law might be going in the next century.

Chapters 1 through 3 are fundamental to understanding everything else in the book, so be sure to read them first. Because so much hinges on documentation in termination cases, I recommend that you also read Chapter 10.

After reading this essential material, however, you can zero in on topics that concern you directly. For instance, if you're having trouble developing a coherent drug testing program, read Chapter 4. If government investigations are your biggest headache, take a look at Chapters 6 and 7. And if a layoff is in the not-too-distant future for your company, go to Chapter 8.

Although *Every Manager's Legal Guide to Firing* is aimed at managers, attorneys can also benefit from reading it, especially Chapters 6 and 7. Your corporate counsel may not specialize in termination law, and the book can help him or her brush up before representing you in a termination case.

Every Manager's Legal Guide to Firing spells out everything you need to know about termination in language that you can understand. My hope is that the book will save you valuable time and keep your legal costs down.

ACKNOWLEDGMENTS

I wish to thank Carmen D. Wiseman for developing and editing this book, Dolores Heidenthal for typing the manuscript, and my wife, Mary Ryan Bequai, and our two children, Christine and William, for their love, support, and patience.

August Bequai

CONTENTS

*Rehabilitation Act of 1973   Title VII of the Civil Rights Act of
1964   State Laws*   Negligence Pitfalls   Employers as
Cops   *Employee Searches   Arrests and Interrogations*   Your Day in
Court   *What It Takes to Win*   A Checklist for
Success   *Planning   Communication   Consent   Handling Abusers*

CHAPTER 1

THE FIRING LINE

"You're fired! Begone, you scoundrel, and never darken the door of this establishment again!" It may sound like dialog from a 19th-century melodrama, but it's how a lot of late-20th-century employers perceive the firing process.

Termination is no longer a matter of simply giving undesirable employees their walking papers. If you doubt me, check out these recent cases.

• When bank officials fired a branch manager, he immediately filed a lawsuit seeking at least $2.5 million in damages. He claimed he was fired in retaliation for his efforts to bring the suspicious activities of other employees to the attention of high-level management.

It turned out that things hadn't been on the up-and-up at the bank; in fact, several employees eventually confessed to involvement in a money laundering scheme. The bank's top-tier managers let the branch manager go in a frantic attempt to keep federal regulatory officials and shareholders who weren't bank employees from finding out about this criminal activity. It never occurred to them that the ex-manager's suit could cause them far more grief than the wrongdoing they had tried to cover up.

• In Los Angeles, the U.S. Justice Department joined forces with an employee who had lost his job for blowing the whistle on a Department of Defense (DoD) contractor. The claimant, a former manager of the contracting company, alleged that the company overcharged the government $25 million for work it did for commercial clients on the same computer system it used for its DoD jobs. The manager did not sue, however, until complaints to company officials and a Pentagon fraud hotline led to his termination. The government jumped in because it thought the case had merit. If that's any indication of how things will go in court, the ex-manager could end up with a hefty sum in damages.

He won't be alone, either. Four out of 10 fired employees who sue their former employers for *wrongful discharge*—a claim that an employee was fired unjustly—usually walk away with settlements of $10,000 to $100,000, according to a survey of the nation's Fortune 1000 companies. In fact, more than half of all terminated employees take some kind of legal action against their former employers. Executives tend to be the most litigious: Some 62 percent of managers who get the axe take their ex-employers to court.

Among the survey's other findings:

1. Employers pay hundreds of thousands of dollars in legal fees for wrongful discharge cases—far more than the amounts they pay in settlements to ex-employees.
2. Two out of three employers cite on-the-job substance abuse as the most serious disciplinary problem leading to termination.
3. To avoid legal challenges to employee dismissals, many companies are offering sizable severance packages in exchange for written releases from future liability. Others have developed internal arbitration procedures for dealing with discipline, termination, and employee grievances.

Until a few years ago, problems between employers and employees usually involved union activity. Now, more than 70 percent of all employment disputes involve wrongful discharge.

There's nothing new about wrongful discharge. What *is* new is the number of ex-employees who are now using it to take financial revenge on former employers.

Face it . . . the old workplace just isn't what it used to be. You may think you have a perfectly good reason to can an employee, but that's not enough any more. If you don't want to find yourself staring down the barrel of a lawsuit after every employee dismissal, you must learn something about the legalities of termination.

You don't have to become a Supreme Court Justice to fire employees. But you do need some grounding in legal basics to see where the termination process might be heading as we approach the 21st century and, most important, to help keep your company from getting clobbered by firing-related litigation.

EMPLOYMENT LAW BASICS

The bedrock of American employment law is the *at-will doctrine*. In the context of termination, at-will means that an employer who has no written contract with an employee can fire that employee at any time, for any reason. Sound familiar? It should—the at-will doctrine has been around for more than a century and is the meat and potatoes of American employment law.

Legislators and the courts, however, have recognized several exceptions to the traditional at-will doctrine. These exceptions and limitations can make firing very sticky for managers and are, as you might have guessed, at the root of a lot of today's workplace-related litigation.

So where does at-will leave off, and where do the exceptions kick in? Before we consider these questions, let's take a closer look at the role at-will plays in the relationship between employer and employee.

Who's the Boss?

Under U.S. law, an employer can be an individual, a partnership, an association, or a corporation. Basically, the employer requires or directs employees to do work. In return, the employees receive wages, salaries, or commissions.

Taken at face value, the employment relationship is pretty straightforward: You do work the way I ask you to do it, and I'll pay you. Of course, nothing in employment law is ever as simple as it seems.

There are, for instance, several different types of employment relationships: at-will relationships, specified-term relationships, and contractual arrangements.

At-Will Relationships.   When there is no oral or written contract specifying the duration of the employment, the employment relationship is considered to be employment-at-will, which I'll cover in more detail later in this chapter. In employment-at-will, either party can terminate the relationship at any time— for any reason, or for no reason at all—unless federal or state laws say otherwise.

Specified-Term Relationships.   A specified-term employee signs an agreement with an employer to perform certain job duties for a designated period. In specified-term employment, it's sometimes hard to determine whether the relationship is between employer and employee, or between client and independent contractor. Legally, this decision depends on several factors: the employer's right to control the employee, the skills required for the job, the length of service, the method of payment, and the intent of both sides. Obviously, the economic and legal ramifications of dealing with contractors differ greatly from those of dealing with employees, so it's worth the trouble to figure out who's who.

Contractual Arrangements.   Many people believe that an employment contract must be a written agreement. Not so! A valid employment contract exists when there is an offer of employment, an acceptance of that offer (a handshake will do), and some kind of payment for services.

Either party can break an employment contract that says nothing about the duration of the employment relationship. In a court case, however, evidence may be introduced to show that the parties *intended* for the employment relationship to continue for a fixed period, or until something happened that would force the relationship to dissolve.

FIRING LAW IN TRANSITION

Well into the 20th century, the employer was the ruler— sometimes benevolent, sometimes despotic—of the workplace. Under the original at-will doctrine, employers couldn't get into trouble over firing if they tried. Discipline and termination were almost God-given rights. Not even an employer who dismissed an employee for refusing to do something morally reprehensible had to worry about a lawsuit.

What was the judicial rationale for this one-sided rule? Mainly, the courts wanted to let employers run their businesses as they saw fit. Taking their cue from the early common law of contracts, the courts hesitated to do anything that would infringe on the freedom of employer and employee to make an employment contract; they tried not to add implicit terms that the two parties might not agree on.

Keeping termination-related lawsuits from bogging down the already strained U.S. judicial system was a concern, too. Even now, jurists worry that relaxing the at-will rule will lead to increased litigation, employers attempting to second-guess the courts on personnel decisions, and a lack of clearly definable standards for judicial review. Some even believe that an eroded at-will doctrine could have an adverse effect on the U.S. economy.

Most of the courts still adhere to the employment-at-will rule in some fashion. Termination law does not start and end with at-will, however. In most areas, established legal doctrine states that an at-will relationship exists unless the length of employment is fixed by a verbal or written agreement. But there are also myriad federal, state, and local laws and regulations that dilute and even reverse the at-will rule. It all boils down to one stark truth: Your right to fire is limited.

EXCEPTIONS TO THE RULE

Guided by the notion that employee dismissals should not violate public policy or otherwise go against the public good in any way, Congress and the courts have have carved out numerous exceptions to the traditional at-will doctrine.

The legislative exceptions expressly forbid employers to fire employees because of their race, sex, age, or religion, or because they are physically challenged. Employers also cannot use termination as a means of getting back at employees who exercise legally guaranteed rights. The judicial exceptions, grounded in contract law and tort theories of liability, generally come under the aegis of wrongful or abusive discharge and unjust dismissal. These exceptions all play a big part in what you can and can't do when you fire or discipline employees.

Legislative Limits

As you probably know, federal fair-employment laws apply to just about every U.S. employer (see Table 1–1). In general, these laws forbid discrimination in any aspect of employment on the basis of race, religion, national origin, or sex. Specific fair-employment laws prevent employers from discriminating against physically challenged employees, limit the use of lie-detector tests in investigating employees, and set strict guidelines for employing aliens.

TABLE 1–1
Federal Fair-Employment Statutes

Civil Rights Act of 1964	Prohibits employers from discriminating on the basis of race, color, religion, sex, or national origin; a 1978 amendment prohibits employers from discriminating on the basis of medical condition, including pregnancy.
National Labor Relations Act	Prohibits employers from engaging in unfair labor practices, such as preventing employees from joining unions, filing complaints with the National Labor Relations Board, or testifying in an NLRB hearing.
Occupational Safety and Health Act	Prohibits employers from discriminating against employees who refuse to work in unsafe conditions, and from firing employees who complain that the workplace does not meet federal health and safety standards.
Age Discrimination in Employment Act	Prohibits employers from discriminating on the basis of age.
Employee Retirement Income Security Act	Prohibits employers from firing employees who participate in employee benefit plans.
Rehabilitation Act of 1973, Americans with Disabilities Act of 1990	Prohibit employers from discriminating against physically or mentally challenged employees who are otherwise qualified for employment.

The federal fair-employment laws are complemented by numerous state laws that put brakes on the employment-at-will rule. The aim of these laws is to protect employees' rights to state safety and health benefits, workers' compensation, and the like. That means you cannot fire or otherwise discriminate against employees for exercising their right to apply for benefits under state law or to testify in proceedings involving, say, workers' compensation claims.

Government agencies tend to be gung ho on antidiscrimination clauses in the contracts they make with private employers. Employers who want to keep their federal or state government contracts will not discipline or fire employees because of color, national origin, sex, or religion.

Many states have adopted the Uniform Trade Secrets Act. This act gives employers the authority to safeguard valuable proprietary information by preventing ex-employees from working for competitors.

How's a manager supposed to keep track of both federal and state employment laws? It's not that hard if you follow a few key laws that affect your right to fire and discipline employees.

Title VII of the Civil Rights Act of 1964. This law, which applies to all employers with 15 or more employees, forbids discrimination because of race, color, religion, sex, or national origin. The act also prohibits:

1. Treatment of a member of a group protected by the act that differs substantially from the way other employees are treated under the same circumstances.
2. Job requirements that disproportionately affect a protected group of employees. (Employers can justify requirements that seem unfair on the surface by demonstrating that such requirements meet legitimate business needs and goals.)
3. Sexual harassment. An employee may sue an employer for creating an "offensive working environment," even if the employee suffers no economic loss. The law demands that employers do whatever is necessary to eliminate sexual harassment in the workplace.

4. Sexual stereotyping. If an employee claims that an employer is using sexual stereotyping as a basis for discrimination in employment, the employer must show that other employers in the industry routinely follow the same practices.

Title VII does not forbid discrimination in employment because of employees' sexual preferences. It does, however, stipulate that pregnancy be viewed the same as any other temporary medical disability.

The act goes out of its way to protect employees who sue their employers for discrimination; it doesn't matter whether the employee's complaint is justified. The Equal Employment Opportunity Commission considers such protection a high-priority item.

If a fired employee wins a discrimination suit under Title VII, the court may order the employer to reinstate the employee in his or her former job. The employer may also have to cough up back pay and attorney fees. (The employee might have to pay attorney fees to the employer, however, if the judge rules that the claim of discrimination is frivolous, unreasonable, or groundless.)

Equal Pay Act of 1963.   This law applies to all employers in the "stream of commerce" (in other words, almost all employers). It requires that male and female employees receive the same pay when jobs involve equivalent skills, effort, and responsibility, and are performed under similar working conditions in the same establishment. Like Title VII, the Equal Pay Act prohibits retaliation against employees who sue their employers under its provisions. Employees who sue and and win may receive back pay and attorney fees, and the court may order a change in the employer's pay policies as well.

Age Discrimination in Employment Act of 1967.   This act, which forbids discrimination against employees aged 40 years or older, applies to employers who have 20 or more employees for each working day in each of 20 or more calendar weeks of the current or preceding calendar year. On January 1, 1987, the age ceiling for protected employees (previously 70 years) was removed.

The act prohibits retaliation against employees who claim discrimination on the basis of age. Employees who win their suits may receive back pay, damages, and attorney fees, and may be reinstated in their former jobs.

Federal Rehabilitation Act of 1973. This act applies to federal agencies and contractors, and to entities that receive financial assistance from the federal government. It protects physically or mentally challenged individuals who are otherwise qualified for employment. If an employee is perceived to be physically or mentally challenged, or has a record of physical or mental disability, the act's protection extends to him or her—even if no impairment actually exists.

Americans with Disabilities Act of 1990. Much like the Federal Rehabilitation Act of 1973, the Americans with Disabilities Act (ADA) prohibits employers from using disability as a basis for firing, refusing to hire, or refusing to promote workers. The key difference between these acts is that the ADA's protection extends to disabled workers in the *private* sector.

The ADA also requires businesses with more than 25 employees to change their physical facilities to accommodate disabled workers within two years. Businesses with 15 to 24 employees have four years to change their facilities. Businesses with fewer than 15 employees are exempt.

Fair Labor Standards Act. This act requires all employers in the stream of commerce to pay a minimum wage, as well as overtime for more than 40 hours of work in a workweek. An employer cannot fire an employee for exercising the rights guaranteed by the act's minimum wage and overtime provisions.

The act does not protect certain employees, including executives, administrative staff, professional staff, and outside salespeople.

Employment Rights of Reservists. This act prevents employers from firing or from denying promotions and other benefits to employees who take time off from work to fulfill their obligations as members of the U.S. military reserves. A reservist who proves discrimination may obtain a court order requiring the employer to reinstate him or her, or to provide illegally denied benefits. Back pay is also an appropriate award.

Under the act, the U.S. Department of Justice has the authority to represent an aggrieved employee if the department is "reasonably satisfied that the person so applying is entitled to such benefits."

Protection for Bankrupt Employees. The U.S. Bankruptcy Code forbids private employers from firing or otherwise discriminating against an employee solely because he or she has filed for bankruptcy. The code also forbids employers from disciplining or maltreating an employee because he or she owes a debt that is payable (or was paid) under the bankruptcy laws.

Immigration Reform and Control Act of 1986. This act requires employers, regardless of the size of their companies, to inspect documents that establish the identity of every newly hired employee and to verify employees' eligibility to work in the United States. It is now against the law to hire an alien who isn't eligible to work in this country. But it is also against the law for employers with four or more employees to fire or otherwise discriminate against a legally registered alien—to use the act as an excuse to get rid of an employee from another country when that employee's papers are in apple-pie order.

Employee Polygraph Protection Act of 1988. This act prevents employers from forcing employees to take a lie-detector or polygraph test except under certain narrowly defined conditions. For example, an employer can request—but not demand—that an employee take a polygraph examination as part of an ongoing investigation of a theft or security threat to the employer's business.

When employee discipline or termination requires polygraph testing, employers must give suspect employees reasonable notice that there is a problem, in advance of the test and *in writing*. The notice must meet these criteria:

1. It must describe the investigation and its purpose.
2. It must mention that the employee had access to the property or information in question.

3. It must give the basis for the employer's suspicions.
4. It must list the questions that the polygraph examiner will ask.

Under the act, an employee can refuse to take a polygraph test or even halt a test in progress without being penalized in any way.

Judicial Constraints

Federal and state courts have also corralled the rights of employers to fire at-will, mostly through the application of contract law.

As I've already mentioned, an employer and employee enter into a legal, binding contract as soon as the employer offers the employee a job and the employee accepts the offer. But an employer may forfeit the power to fire at-will if he or she makes an agreement that limits the rights of both parties to dissolve their contractual relationship. If employer and employee have such an arrangement and the employer breaks the contract by firing the employee, the employee can sue for wrongful discharge.

Among the several types of employment contracts are implied contracts, express contracts, and definite contracts.

Implied Contracts

Not all contracts say everything in so many words. Sometimes what you imply makes a stronger impression than what you think you're saying. Even an implied contract, however, is legally binding.

For example, an employer may appear to promise job security by telling a worker that she will never be terminated as long as her job performance is satisfactory. The employer may not actually come right out and say that the employee will always have a job. Still, the employer's words and actions during recruitment interviews, personnel orientations, and so on lead the employee to believe that her job will be safe forever. If she is terminated for a reason other than poor performance, she is likely to remember the implicit promise of job security and sue the employer. And, it's likely that she'll win—the courts are forcing more and more employers to live up to their implied contracts in such cases.

Express Contracts

An express contract is the opposite of an implied one: It states *everything* in writing. Thus, if an express contract says that an employer gives up his or her right to fire at-will, the judge doesn't need to know more. In general, though, the courts won't uphold even an express contract that restrains trade, offends a widely accepted public policy, or breaks a law.

Definite Contracts

An employment contract for a specified period can be broken only for a good reason, and only during the term of the contract. If no definite period of employment is stated or implied, employment for a monthly or annual salary is presumed to be employment at-will. Of course, both the employer and the employee can get out of an employment-at-will arrangement at any time without running the risk of being sued for breach of contract.

From the employer's standpoint, a definite contract isn't a great idea. Even contracts that offer employment at a specific annual salary or provide for annual salary reviews can trip you up. Because such a contract states a unit of time to set the employee's compensation or review period, the court may interpret the contract as saying that you meant the job to last only for that unit of time.

It's worth noting that the courts do not consider employment for life, permanent employment, or employment until retirement to be employment for a definite term.

A growing number of courts are embracing the idea that employee handbooks represent *unilateral contracts*. In fact, most states allow a terminated employee to sue for breach of contract if an employee handbook, personnel manual, or similar company policy document gives assurances of job security. Likewise, a judge will probably make a company follow its layoff and recall-to-work policies as stated in the company's employee handbook.

Clearly, the judicial trend is toward treating employee manuals and personnel documents as binding contracts. In a typical termination case involving such materials, the courts will also try to answer these questions:

1. Did the employer follow a publicly announced policy of encouraging long-term employment?
2. Did the employer generally fire employees only for good reasons ("for cause")?
3. Did the employer assure the employee verbally that he or she could be fired only for cause?
4. Did the employee handbook offer the employee a written assurance that he or she could be fired only for cause?

An employee handbook doesn't have to be a loaded gun. You can stave off handbook-related termination hassles by inserting disclaimers in your employment application form, personnel materials, or both.

Putting a disclaimer in your application form lets employees know from the start that they are employed at-will; thus, they will be unable to use your employee handbook as proof of a unilateral contract in firing disputes. To defuse the employee handbook threat once and for all, insert an employment-at-will disclaimer in the handbook itself—and make sure it appears in all revised versions!

Given the importance of contracts in employment law, it's not surprising that many employees use *interference with contractual relations* as grounds for suing their former bosses. (Remember, a contract can be any verbal or written agreement.)

Some employers confuse interference with contractual relations and breach of contract. Although both can put you in the hot seat, there are differences between the two legal concepts.

In an interference suit, there must be a valid contractual or business relationship between employer and employee, and the employer must acknowledge that such a relationship exists. If the employee wants to win the suit, he or she must show that the employer intentionally did something to perturb or break the relationship, thereby hurting the employee. The employee does not have to prove malice on the employer's part, just knowledge of the contractual relationship and intent to interfere with it.

Courts in several states now recognize that there is an implied "covenant of good faith and fair dealing" in employment contracts, even in employment-at-will relationships. This covenant assumes that neither side will do anything to hinder the other from receiving the contract's benefits.

MORE LEGAL TRAPS FOR EMPLOYERS

Breach of contract isn't the only ace in the hole for ex-employees who sue their employers in wrongful discharge actions. Other widely used legal gambits include accusing the employer of fraud, "detrimental reliance," violation of public policy, infliction of emotional distress, defamation, assault and battery, or negligence.

Fraud

Joe S. leaves his job at Foobaron International to take a supposedly better position at Zagnut, Inc. Zagnut has enticed Joe with promises of great pay, five weeks of vacation a year, and many other wonderful benefits. Not long after Joe comes on board at Zagnut, however, the company decides to let him go. Joe feels that he's been bilked, that Zagnut has lured him away from Foobaron under false pretenses. Not surprisingly, he decides to sue Zagnut for fraud.

To win such a suit, an employee must provide clear, convincing evidence that an employer knowingly misrepresented a crucial fact to the employee, with the aim of misleading him or her. The employee must also show that he or she was hurt in some way as a result of believing the employer's fraudulent promises.

Detrimental Reliance

Occasionally an employer asks an employee to do something far beyond the call of duty—to drop a personal injury claim against the company, to move to another residence, to invest in the company, to resign from government service, or to give up his or her own business. In return, the employer offers to give the employee a raise or other reward.

There will certainly be trouble if the employer doesn't come through with the promised reward. And if the employer fires the employee for refusing, say, to drop the personal injury claim, there will be even more trouble. As far as the courts are concerned, the firing ends the employment-at-will relationship, and the employer can be sued for *detrimental reliance* (so called because the employee has relied, to his or her detriment, on the employer's word). Employers who try to get more out of their employees than an honest day's work should protect themselves against the possibility of detrimental reliance suits.

Public Policy

The courts, like the federal and state legislatures, will not tolerate anything that goes against public policy—what society considers legally, and often morally, right. In termination law, public policy exceptions to the at-will rule include:

1. Firing an employee for refusing to violate a criminal statute, such as a law forbidding deceptive business practices.
2. Firing an employee for exercising a right guaranteed by law, such as the right to file a workers' compensation claim.
3. Firing an employee for fulfilling a legal duty, such as serving on a jury.
4. Firing an employee for reporting alleged violations of the law, such as blowing the whistle on problems at a nuclear plant or telling health officials about a shipment of adulterated food.
5. Firing an employee for refusing to violate a generally accepted public policy, such as the prohibition against lying or doing something that puts others in peril. Thus, an employer cannot dismiss an employee for refusing to lie to save a supervisor's neck or for disregarding orders to increase production at a nuclear plant to dangerous levels.
6. Firing an employee for exercising rights guaranteed by the First Amendment (the Bill of Rights), such as the right to disagree with managerial ideology.

Defamation

It's part of human nature, I guess, that employers make nasty
comments when they fire employees. Some managers just can't
pass up the opportunity to tell the employee they're firing exactly
what they think of him or her. Others nail an ex-employee to the
wall when they explain to the rest of the staff why he or she was
terminated. Such remarks can lead to tremendous legal problems if the subject of the unflattering remarks decides to haul the
employer into court for *defamation*.

Legally, defamation refers to the dissemination of false or
derogatory statements about an individual. It's one of the most
common legal vehicles used by plaintiffs in termination cases.

Most jurisdictions give employers a *qualified privilege* to
spread otherwise derogatory information about employees if
there's a legitimate business reason. Under the law, anyone can
make a "qualified privileged communication" about any subject,
as long as the communicator honestly believes that he or she has
a duty to pass on the information to others with the same interests or obligations. For example, an employer might feel compelled to warn other employers about an employee who is caught
stealing company property.

An employee can't sue you even for making a *false* statement
protected by a qualified privilege if you make the statement
without malice. But you're no longer making a qualified privileged communication if you spread nasty rumors that you don't
believe yourself about an employee, or if you broadcast derogatory information out of spite, ill-will, or other less than sterling
motives.

Another defamation loophole lets employers pass on information to employees in the company for business purposes. So, if
you fire an employee and then tell other members of his or her
department (that is, people who really need to know about the
dismissal) in calm, temperate language, you can't be accused of
defamation.

Be careful, however, about whom you tell and how you tell it.
An employer can't really claim qualified privilege if he or she
spreads information based on an anonymous letter (whose contents are dubious at best and a lie at worst) to everyone in the
division.

Emotional Distress

An employee may claim that being fired has caused him or her extreme embarrassment, humiliation, or trauma, and may try to sue for *infliction of emotional distress*. The employee stands a reasonable chance of winning the suit if:

1. The employer has intentionally or recklessly harmed the employee. The courts say that a claim satisfies this condition if the employer actually meant to inflict distress, or if the employer should have known that distress would result.
2. The employer's behavior has been so intolerable that it offends generally accepted standards of decency and morality. The aim of this condition is to prevent frivolous suits and to head off litigation in situations involving only bad manners and bruised feelings.
3. The emotional distress is severe.
4. The employer's behavior actually caused the employee's emotional distress.

Termination itself is not the sort of "extreme and outrageous conduct" that would elicit an emotional-distress ruling in the employee's favor. An employee can't claim emotional distress just because he or she was fired.

Assault and Battery

There's no doubt that firing is an emotional process. Tempers can fray on both sides of the desk, and sometimes a few fists fly as well. But the blows don't really hit home until a terminated employee pops an employer with an assault and battery suit.

Nowadays, terminated employees most often charge assault and battery in cases involving sexual harassment. The latest trend is employees charging supervisors with "offensive" touching. Watch out! Your company may be liable for sexual assault and battery committed by supervisory employees, particularly if they otherwise did their jobs the way they were supposed to.

Constructive Discharge

Some bosses would rather eat ground glass than fire an employee, so they apply pressure—sometimes subtle, sometimes not—on the employee to resign. I think even timid bosses would agree, however, that firing someone is infinitely preferable to a *constructive discharge* lawsuit.

To prove constructive discharge, an employee must show that the employer deliberately tried to get him or her to quit, making working conditions intolerable. Intent is the key in determining whether the employer's actions were deliberate. The objective test for evaluating intolerable working conditions is simple: Would any other reasonable person have felt compelled to quit if he or she had been in the employee's shoes?

Sneak Attacks

Even if an ex-employee can't go after an employer for breaking a contract or for sexual harassment, he or she still has plenty of legal ammunition. It's hard to protect yourself against such suits, because the legal concepts they embody aren't very obvious.

Did you ever think that filling out a performance evaluation could get you sued for *negligence*? It can happen if an employee believes that a shoddily done evaluation led to his or her termination.

How about *conspiracy* charges? Believe it or not, a terminated employee could sue you for, say, conspiring with others in your company to injure his or her reputation, trade, business, or profession.

In a civil conspiracy, two or more people get together to do something illegal or to use illegal means to accomplish a legal purpose, resulting in damage to the employee. There can be no conspiracy, however, in an employment-at-will relationship.

You can even get in trouble for *not* firing an employee! Let's say you hire a worker who is on probation for aggravated sexual assault. If that worker assaults a co-worker, you can be sued for *negligent hiring,* especially if you didn't check his background carefully before you took him on. If you don't fire this employee, who obviously poses a threat to his fellow workers, you can be sued for *negligent retention*. You may also be found guilty of negligent retention if you don't terminate an incompetent contractor who consistently botches jobs, or an embezzling supervisor.

THINK BEFORE YOU FIRE

Your Victorian counterparts had it easy. If a 19th-century boss didn't like something an employee said, that employee had to hit the road. Now that the legislatures and courts have carved up the at-will doctrine like a Thanksgiving turkey, there's a lot more to firing than showing a problem employee to the door.

As you've seen, ex-employees are ingenious at coming up with ways to stick it to their former employers in court. And more and more courts are awarding punitive damages to employees in wrongful discharge cases, particularly in suits involving public policy exceptions to the at-will doctrine.

The best defense is offense. Stay on top of what's happening in employment law, and try to figure out how changes in the law affect your organization. Periodically review your recruitment policies, orientation and training programs, employee handbooks and personnel materials, and, of course, discharge policies and practices. Remember: An offhand remark during a recruitment interview or an ambiguous passage in an employee handbook can spark a long, expensive, ugly termination suit.

You'll be off to a good start if you keep one thing in mind:

Federal and state laws, and court rulings, limit what you can and can't do when you fire employees.

CHAPTER 2

HOW PERSONNEL LAWS
REALLY WORK

You now have the theoretical and conceptual basics of termination law under your belt. In fact, you may already know more about the subject than many lawyers! But is this newfound wisdom enough to keep you out of court when you have to discipline or fire problem employees? Not quite.

Termination law is no different than any other kind: There's theory, and there's real life. In theory, the at-will doctrine lets you fire anyone you want to. In practice, you have to walk softly—and forget about carrying a big stick.

No one law prohibits you or any other private employer from terminating or disciplining employees without good cause. But there are plenty of federal laws that prevent you from firing employees because of age, physical or mental disability, sex, union involvement, even wage garnishment. You can't fire employees for filing complaints or assisting with procedures related to enforcing these laws, either.

To add even more spice to the stew, some states and cities have passed laws that forbid employers to discipline or fire workers for performing jury duty, filing workers' compensation claims, or refusing to take lie-detector tests. Others have barred employers from discriminating against employees because of marital status or sexual preference.

Challenging terminations and disciplinary actions in court has become a favorite pastime of American employees. More court cases mean increased restrictions on your right to fire. For instance, state courts have ruled in favor of employees who were dismissed for refusing to commit perjury, to approve market testing of a possibly harmful drug, or to date a supervisor. In other decisions, employees have won when their employers fired them to avoid having to pay big commissions, or when employers reneged on implied promises of long-term employment.

Learning how personnel laws work in theory will get you a good grade in Employment Law 101. Learning how these laws work in the real world will help you develop termination policies that do what you want them to do without putting your organization in the hot seat.

Throughout this chapter, you may find yourself asking what a particular law has to do with discipline and termination. The answer is simple: *Every* aspect of employment law has something to do with discipline and termination! You never know when some savvy attorney will turn an innocent-looking act against you in court, so it's important to know the key laws and understand how they might affect you. It's all part of how the employment game is really played.

THE DISCRIMINATION GAME

Over the past couple of decades, Congress and the states have produced a bumper crop of legislation designed to further equal employment opportunity for all qualified workers. These anti-discrimination laws may be the most important development on the American employment scene since the eight-hour workday.

Title VII of the Civil Rights Act of 1964 is the cornerstone of equal employment opportunity. It prohibits discrimination in employment on the basis of race, color, religion, sex, or national origin.

Title VII affects every term and condition of employment, from the help-wanted ad to the exit interview. For instance, the law requires that you train and promote workers in all job classifications without discrimination. You must base promotion decisions on valid job requirements, and you must offer training and apprenticeship opportunities that are in line with equal employment principles. An employer is in big trouble if he or she finds some flimsy reason to terminate, say, an African-American employee who would otherwise be climbing the corporate ladder.

But Title VII doesn't cover all the bases. Congress has had to pass additional laws to protect vulnerable groups such as older workers, the physically and mentally challenged, women, and union members.

Never Too Old

After 25 years as a bank teller, Betty L. was unceremoniously fired. She thought that her impending 50th birthday might have had something to do with the sudden termination. A Labor Department investigation revealed that one of the bank's high-level personnel officers had told Betty's supervisor that Betty was too old to be a teller; the bank was trying to liven up its image, and it wanted "cute, young things" behind the teller windows. The supervisor followed the party line and gave Betty a bad performance review; after all, he didn't want to lose *his* job.

An investigation turned up other evidence of age discrimination at the bank. An ad had been placed in the local newspapers for a "young person" to fill Betty's position. A job order had been sent to an employment agency for teller trainees between the ages of 21 and 24. And, none of the new tellers hired was older than 30. Eventually, a judge ordered the bank to rehire Betty and give her substantial back pay.

This is a prime example of how employers can get clobbered by the Age Discrimination in Employment Act (ADEA). The ADEA is a law with very long arms. It covers all government employers, private employers with 20 or more employees, employment agencies serving employers to which the ADEA applies, and labor unions with more than 25 members.

If your organization falls into any of these categories, you cannot fire, refuse to promote or hire, or otherwise discriminate against an individual simply because of his or her age. Neither can you deny older employees benefits such as life or health insurance. The law also prevents the employment agencies you deal with from refusing to refer qualified older applicants to your company, and it keeps labor unions from using age as an excuse to exclude or expel members.

As Betty's case shows, employers are cruising for a bruising if they think they can sidestep the ADEA by running help-wanted ads for young workers after firing older ones. The act specifically prohibits advertisements that indicate a preference for younger employees or that promote other forms of age discrimination. Thus, an ad calling for applicants between the ages of 25 and 45 directly violates the ADEA.

The act does not apply to employment in which age is a bona fide occupational qualification, such as modeling junior miss fashions, or to registered apprenticeship programs. Also, if a job is physically taxing, you may ask older employees to undergo medical examinations to ensure that they're up to the demands of the work. And, the ADEA doesn't stop you from disciplining or firing an older worker for a good reason.

Age requirements for legitimate seniority systems aren't a problem under the ADEA, nor are employee retirement, pension, or insurance plans. However, the act prohibits using employee benefit systems as a means of "retiring" supposedly undesirable older workers.

How does the ADEA work? Let's say that 60-year-old copyeditor John B. believes that he's been "retired early" from Zagnut Publishing because the company wants to bring in new blood. John begins the process by filing a complaint with the Equal Employment Opportunity Commission (EEOC; see box, "The EEOC in Action"), which enforces the ADEA. After receiving notice of a possible ADEA violation, an equal opportunity specialist interviews John to find out what happened and to counsel him about his rights under the law.

The equal opportunity specialist tries to mediate (conciliate) between John and Zagnut, but can't get the two parties to reach an informal agreement. The EEOC decides to investigate further. Eventually it discovers that Zagnut is quietly easing older employees out of their jobs, especially those who've been with the company a long time and have a lot of accrued benefits. Clearly Zagnut is violating the ADEA, so the EEOC takes the company to court—where John stands a good chance of coming out on top.

Like most discrimination laws, the ADEA makes it illegal for employers to penalize employees for initiating proceedings under the act, opposing employment practices that promote age discrimination, participating in EEOC investigations, or testifying in ADEA-related court cases.

The EEOC in Action

What should you expect when an employee thinks that you have treated him or her unfairly because of sex, race, color, religion, or national origin? In many cases, the employee will file a complaint or charge with the Equal Employment Opportunity Commission (EEOC) or a comparable state or local agency.

Initiating a complaint is simple. The complaint form merely requires the name and address of both the employee and the employer, plus a brief description of the discriminatory practice or action.

The complaint must be filed within 180 days of the occurrence of the problem. If there is a state or city fair employment practices law offering comparable protection (42 states have such laws), the EEOC may send a copy of the complaint to the agency responsible for enforcing the state or local law. If the state agency does not take action on the complaint within 60 days, the EEOC may begin processing the charge.

When the employee files the initial complaint with the state agency, the deadline for filing with EEOC is 300 days from the date of the alleged illegal act or within 30 days of a notice that the state agency has finished its proceedings, whichever comes first. Complaints that involve continuing violations of Title VII aren't subject to the usual time limits.

Let's say that the EEOC decides to pay attention to a discrimination complaint from one of your employees. First, it sends an equal opportunity specialist to talk to the employee. The specialist fills out the charge form, provides counseling on the employee's legal rights, and explains the EEOC enforcement process. After filing the charge, the EEOC notifies you; it may ask you to come to the commission office to discuss the charge with the EEOC staff.

If the EEOC cannot settle the complaint through conciliation efforts, it will investigate further to determine whether discrimination has occurred. Then EEOC attorneys will review the case again. If there is a strong indication of discrimination against the employee, the lawyers will probably recommend that the EEOC sue you. Otherwise, the EEOC will give the employee a right-to-sue letter that permits him or her to file a private lawsuit against you.

(*concluded*)

The employee doesn't have to wait for this entire process to end before he or she files a private suit. He or she can file a suit any time after the 180 days allotted to the EEOC to consider the discrimination complaint. But the employee must have a right-to-sue letter before initiating any court action. Once the employee has the right-to-sue letter, he or she has 90 days to file in court.

The ADEA isn't the only weapon in the older employee's arsenal. With the graying of the influential Baby Boom generation, many states have also passed age discrimination laws or included provisions in their fair employment practices laws that prohibit discrimination based on age. Some of these laws place no ceiling on age discrimination in employment; others protect workers until they reach 60, 65, or 70 years of age.

What's a Handicap?

Few aspects of employment have changed as dramatically as employers' attitudes toward employees with physical or mental disabilities. Of course, these new, enlightened attitudes owe much to federal and state regulations mandating equal opportunity for the disabled.

Section 503 of the Rehabilitation Act of 1973 protects physically and mentally challenged employees against discrimination, but only if they work for federal contractors and subcontractors who hold contracts greater than $2,500. If a physically or mentally challenged individual is otherwise qualified to do a job, the contractor cannot use the disability as an excuse to fire him or her. Section 503 also applies to hiring, promotions, compensation—in a nutshell, all terms and conditions of employment.

The Office of Federal Contract Compliance Programs (OFCCP), a part of the U.S. Department of Labor, enforces section 503 of the Rehabilitation Act. The OFCCP's affirmative action guidelines require contractors and subcontractors to actively recruit physically and mentally challenged individuals, and to make reasonable efforts to accommodate disabled employees.

Some courts have held that individuals can sue under section 503; others have stated that only the federal government can take action against its contractors. When the OFCCP gets a disability discrimination complaint from either source, it investigates the problem and attempts to mediate between the worker and the contractor. The OFCCP may eventually take the contractor to court for violating section 503.

The government may withhold payments from a contractor found guilty of discriminating against disabled workers. The contractor also faces the possibility of being "defrocked" and losing the chance to bid on future government contracts.

A 1978 amendment to section 504 of the Rehabilitation Act forbids programs or activities receiving federal funds from discriminating against physically or mentally challenged employees. Individuals can take legal action against such programs for discriminatory acts. The agency providing the federal funds is responsible for enforcing section 504, with help from the Department of Justice and the EEOC.

Bolstering the Rehabilitation Act are federal regulations, also enforced by the EEOC, that prohibit government agencies from discriminating against otherwise qualified physically or mentally challenged workers. Public employers must reasonably accommodate the known physical or mental limitations of qualified employees, and must also issue guidelines on the acceptance and processing of discrimination complaints.

Before the summer of 1990, only federal employers or contractors really had to worry about being sued for discriminating against disabled workers. Although the fair employment practices laws of many states were tough on employers who discriminated against physically or mentally challenged individuals, there was no federal statute to safeguard the employment rights of the disabled.

That has changed with the passage of the landmark Americans with Disabilities Act (ADA) of 1990. The act prohibits discrimination against the disabled in employment, public accommodations, transportation, and telecommunications. And it particularly targets private-sector employers.

The ADA, like the Federal Rehabilitation Act of 1973, forbids private employers from firing or refusing to hire any worker because of his or her disability. Being physically or mentally challenged is no longer an appropriate reason to bar an otherwise qualified applicant from a job.

Also like its public-sector counterpart, the ADA demands that private businesses reasonably accommodate disabled workers. Companies with more than 15 but fewer than 25 employees have up to four years to change their physical plants. Companies with more than 25 employees have only two years to modify their facilities. This requirement, however, does not apply to businesses with fewer than 15 workers.

You might also be exempt from the requirement to provide reasonable accommodation to disabled workers if you can prove that making the ADA-mandated changes would be too expensive, disruptive, or burdensome, or would substantially alter the way you do business. Moreover, you do not have to retrofit existing buildings or transportation vehicles if the renovation effort proves too costly or difficult.

Working Women

Despite the growing number of female employees in the U.S. work force, women still make only about two thirds the salary of their male counterparts in many jobs. Some male managers try to prevent female employees from scaling the corporate hierarchy or to extort sexual favors from them. If things aren't changing quickly, however, it's not due to lack of legislative effort. Several federal laws have the goal of ensuring equal employment opportunity and pay equity for women, while others protect against sexual harassment in the workplace.

Equal Pay Act of 1963
Purepillz, a pharmaceutical company, pays male bottlers 50 cents an hour more than it pays female bottlers. Purepillz tries to justify the pay differential by claiming that the men have to lift heavy boxes of bottled medications. When a female employee protests the unequal wage rates, a company representative tells her that she is welcome to look for a higher salary elsewhere. The worker sues Purepillz, and eventually the case winds up in fed-

eral court. The judge rules against the company, noting that under the Federal Equal Pay Act of 1963, "equal" does not mean identical—it means *substantially* equal.

The Equal Pay Act prohibits employers from creating differential pay scales for women and men who work in the same establishment and whose jobs demand the same skill, effort, and responsibility. Employers cannot reduce the wage rate of employees as a means of eliminating the illegal wage differentials, either. The act does permit pay differences based on a seniority or merit system, or on a system that measures earnings by quantity or quality of production.

The Equal Pay Act affects just about every U.S. worker. It probably affects you! Under the act, "wages" are all employment-related payments, including overtime, uniforms, travel, and fringe benefits. Moreover, the law applies to federal, state, and local government employees; executive, administrative, and professional employees; and outside salespeople.

As the Purepillz case demonstrates, men's and women's jobs don't have to be absolutely identical. In assessing "equal work," the courts usually consider job descriptions or classifications irrelevant unless they accurately reflect job content. But the courts do take into account the mental effort demanded by a job, as well as the physical labor.

Donna P. thinks she is not receiving equal pay for her work as a carpenter on a construction site. The site supervisor says she doesn't work as hard or long as the male carpenters. Donna disagrees; heated words are exchanged. The supervisor tells her that if she doesn't like what she's earning, she can take a hike.

Donna files a complaint with the EEOC, which enforces the Equal Pay Act. The EEOC finds that the construction company has indeed violated the law by paying Donna less than male carpenters doing 90 percent of the same work. After the EEOC negotiates a settlement with the construction company, Donna gets back pay and the company raises its pay scales so that all female construction workers receive exactly the same wages as male workers doing comparable tasks. If the company hadn't been willing to settle, the EEOC would have filed a suit to collect Donna's back wages.

Donna might have done even better than she did: Under the

act, employees can sue employers for damages, attorney's fees, and court costs as well as back pay. Because Donna received back pay by EEOC order, however, she gave up her right to sue the construction company, as she would have if the EEOC had initiated court proceedings to obtain back pay for her.

An employee must file suit within two years of an Equal Pay Act violation. If an employer intentionally violates the act, however, the employee gets three years to file.

"Women's Work" and Title VII

Despite the rise of women in many high-powered occupations formerly dominated by men, the "pink-collar" employment ghetto refuses to go away. The percentage of women in secretarial and clerical work, teaching, nursing, and the like remains high while the wages for these jobs remain dismally low. That's because of the widespread perception that pink-collar jobs require less education, experience, skill, and responsibility than just about any work done by men.

Some women who work in pink-collar occupations have filed complaints under Title VII of the Civil Rights Act. They've charged that their work is undervalued and underpaid; just about any job seems to merit a higher salary when men do it. In response, the Supreme Court has ruled that the Title VII prohibition against sex-based wage discrimination does not apply only to claims of equal pay for equal work. Nurses have used this ruling to claim that they should not be paid less than city garbage collectors. And clerical workers have used it to show that they receive less money than physical plant employees because of sexual stereotyping.

This area of the law is still developing. So far, the courts have not precisely determined the boundaries of sex-based wage discrimination under Title VII. Sooner or later they'll come to a conclusion, however, so don't make the mistake of paying female administrative assistants less because they do "women's work."

Executive Order 11246

The federal government may occasionally have trouble getting private employers to provide equal employment opportunity to all deserving workers, but the government is good at making its contractors toe the antidiscrimination line. There's a strong incentive to do the right thing: If contractors discriminate in employment, they may lose their contracts.

Executive Order 11246 forbids employment discrimination based on sex, race, color, religion, or national origin. It affects all federal service and supply contractors and subcontractors, as well as companies holding a federal or federally assisted construction contract of $10,000 or more.

In most cases, the order applies to all of the contractor's facilities, even if they're not involved in providing supplies or services to fulfill the contract. But if a state or local government has a federal contract, the order applies only to the agency involved in the contract. The exceptions here are educational institutions and medical facilities.

Under Executive Order 11246, federal contractors must take affirmative action in recruiting women and members of minority groups. Likewise, they cannot discriminate in hiring new employees; in upgrading, demoting, or transferring current employees; or in selecting employees for training programs and apprenticeships. Pay scales and other compensation must be completely equitable. And, needless to say, contractors cannot lay off or fire employees for discriminatory reasons.

The OFCCP enforces Executive Order 11246, as it does the Rehabilitation Act of 1973. The OFCCP sets policy and develops regulations for implementing the order, and checks to see that federal contractors comply with these regulations. Compliance reviews are the primary mechanism for carrying out the federal government's equal employment policies.

OFCCP sex discrimination guidelines stipulate, among other things, that federal contractors cannot:

1. Run recruitment ads in the "Help Wanted–Male" or "Help Wanted–Female" section of the classifieds.
2. Base seniority rosters on sex.
3. Deny a person a job because of state "protective" labor laws stating, for example, that women cannot work in dangerous occupations.
4. Make distinctions between married or unmarried persons of one sex but not the other.

An employee cannot sue a contracting company for violating Executive Order 11246. But he or she can drop in to an OFCCP office or file a discrimination complaint with the OFCCP by phone or letter. Also, individuals and organizations can file complaints on behalf of workers who have been discriminated against by federal contractors. A complaint letter must describe the discriminatory action, give the names and addresses of the contractor and of all individuals affected by the discrimination, and provide any other pertinent information that might help the OFCCP investigate the problem.

A complaint must be filed no more than 180 days after the discriminatory action occurs. The OFCCP won't extend the filing time unless the complainant has an ironclad reason for being late.

After receiving a complaint, the OFCCP may refer it to the EEOC if it involves discrimination against only one person. But if the complaint describes discriminatory employment practices that affect many workers, the OFCCP will probably forge ahead and investigate. The agency's primary concern is discrimination against large chunks of a contractor's work force.

When an investigation indicates that a federal contractor has violated Executive Order 11246, the OFCCP tries to reach a *conciliation agreement*. Under the terms of such an agreement, the contractor might have to pay back wages or give promotions to employees who have been discriminated against.

If the conciliation attempt fails, the errant contractor must then go through an established administrative process, including a formal hearing. Contractors who don't play by the rules may have their payments withheld, lose their contracts, or be barred from future federal contract work.

Sexual Harassment

Larry I., playboy extraordinaire, just can't seem to keep his "Russian hands and Roman fingers" off the female account executives he supervises. Most of the time, he's just obnoxiously touchy-feely; the women complain, but they put up with the friendly little pats and double entendres because they want to keep their jobs. One day, however, Larry promises attractive salesperson Karin R. a choice sales territory and a big increase in commissions if she meets him at the No-Tell Motel after work. She tells him to take a long walk off a short pier. He fires her. She returns the favor by suing Larry and his company under Title VII of the Civil Rights Act, which states that sexual harassment is an illegal employment practice.

The EEOC stipulates that unwelcome sexual advances, requests for sexual favors, and other verbal or physical conduct of a sexual nature constitute sexual harassment when:

1. A supervisor implies or explicitly demands that an employee submit to sexual advances as a condition of employment.
2. A supervisor uses submission to or rejection of sexual advances as the basis for employment decisions affecting an employee.
3. A supervisor's sexual behavior unreasonably interferes with an employee's job performance or creates an intimidating, hostile, or offensive work environment.

Under the EEOC guidelines, employers, employment agencies, joint apprenticeship committees, and labor organizations are responsible for the actions of their supervisory employees and agents. Ignorance is no shield: Your company is still liable if an oversexed supervisor makes a pass at an employee, even if you knew nothing about the supervisor's activities

Let's change the scenario slightly. George N. works in the same department as Nancy T. George's role model is Larry I.; he thinks Larry is a man's man, a real stud. One day at the office, George tries to prove how much of a stud he is by grabbing a strategic portion of Nancy T.'s anatomy and asking her to go to the No-Tell Motel with him. Nancy is horrified. She sues the company, claiming that George's sexual harassment has created an offensive atmosphere, making it difficult for her to do her job. What's going on?

Well, the EEOC says you're also responsible for curbing sexual harassment of employees by their co-workers. (In some cases, you might even be responsible for sexual harassment of employees by clients or customers.) However, you're off the hook if you had no way of knowing about the employee's behavior or if you did something about the problem right away.

An employee who believes that he or she has been sexually harassed can file a Title VII sex discrimination complaint with the EEOC. A victim of sexual harassment can also file a suit under state laws designed to protect against assault and battery, intentional infliction of emotional distress, or intentional interference with an employment contract.

Women's Health Issues

Jerri H. takes a leave of absence from her job as a marketing coordinator at Mulm and Mulm to have a baby. When she returns to work, she is given a temporary position as a marketing assistant. Worse, her accrued seniority benefits seem to have evaporated, so she no longer has a chance of vying for a permanent job.

Jerri learns that Michael K., who took a leave of absence to recuperate from a major operation, still has his seniority benefits. Smelling a rat, Jerri sues the company and wins. The court states that Mulm and Mulm's policy toward pregnant employees clearly violates Title VII of the Civil Rights Act of 1964.

A 1978 amendment to Title VII prohibits discrimination because of pregnancy. Here's what you cannot do:

1. Refuse to employ a woman because she is pregnant.
2. Fire a woman for being pregnant.
3. Force a woman to go on leave at an arbitrary point during her pregnancy.
4. Deny a pregnant employee credit for previous service, accrued retirement benefits, or accumulated seniority.

Title VII, however, does not demand that you provide a specific number of weeks for maternity leave, that you give pregnant women preferential treatment in hiring or promotions, or that you establish a new medical leave-of-absence or benefits program if none currently exists. Basically, the law states that you should treat female employees affected by pregnancy, childbirth, or related medical conditions exactly the same as you treat other employees who have the same ability or inability to work.

In some states, pregnant workers are entitled to benefits under statewide temporary disability insurance laws, special sections of fair employment or labor codes, and regulations or court decisions imposing statutory bans on sex discrimination in employment.

The amendment to Title VII does not require you to pay health insurance benefits for abortions unless the mother's life is in danger or medical problems have resulted from an abortion. On the other hand, it doesn't stop you from providing abortion benefits.

No matter how you personally feel about the issue, you cannot fire or refuse to hire a woman for having an abortion. Unless the Supreme Court does an about-face on *Roe* v. *Wade*, a woman has the right to get an abortion if she chooses.

Be Fair to Unions

Managers with an inflated sense of their own power may threaten to discipline or fire employees who try to organize a union. What these bosses don't realize is that discrimination against union supporters or members is patently illegal under the National Labor Relations Act (NLRA). The NLRA, as amended by the Labor-Management Relations Act, gives employees the right to form, join, or aid labor unions; to bargain collectively, through representatives of their choice, about wages, hours, and other terms of employment; and to participate in strikes, work stoppages, and similar activities to secure better working conditions.

The NLRA also designates certain labor practices as unfair. Prohibited employer activities include:

1. Interfering with employees' rights to organize, join, or become involved with a labor organization.
2. Interfering with the formation or administration of a labor organization.
3. Preventing employees from making financial contributions to or otherwise supporting labor organizations.
4. Implementing discriminatory hiring procedures, tenure rules, or terms and conditions of employment that encourage or discourage membership in a labor organization.

5. Firing or discriminating against employees for filing charges or testifying under the NLRA.
6. Refusing to participate in collective bargaining.

Employees also have a guaranteed right not to join a union or participate in union activities unless union membership is a requirement for employment. Some states have right-to-work laws that forbid making union membership a prerequisite for employment. In states that do permit union shops to impose membership requirements, employees usually have a grace period of at least 30 days after being hired to become a union member.

The NLRA does not apply to agricultural laborers, private household workers, independent contractors, supervisors, railroad workers, government employees, and some hospital workers.

THE HAZARDS GAME

There's a scene in *The Jungle* by Upton Sinclair in which a slaughterhouse worker accidentally falls into a vat of entrails and is quickly processed into sausage. This horrific accident was possible in the early 20th century, when there were no legal constraints on employers to provide a safe working environment for their employees. Nowadays, however, myriad federal and state laws regulate the conditions under which employees work—and not complying with them may prove hazardous to your business's health.

Foremost among these laws is the Occupational Safety and Health Act (OSHA) of 1970. OSHA's goal is to ensure a safe and healthy working environment; it states that your workplace must be free from recognized hazards that might cause death or serious physical harm.

OSHA is a far-reaching law that applies to employers in all businesses "affecting commerce." The only exceptions are industries such as mining, which have their own health and safety regulations, and public employers, whose workers are covered by a special executive order. The states, operating under a plan approved by the federal government, usually cover both state and local government employees.

The Occupational Safety and Health Administration, an arm of the Department of Labor, establishes standards for conditions and practices required to protect workers on the job. It's your responsibility to learn and comply with these standards, to put them into effect, and to make sure that employees have and use equipment to protect themselves in hazardous work situations.

If your employees believe that you're not holding up your end, they can:

1. Ask OSHA to conduct an inspection to determine if there are hazardous conditions or standards violations in their workplace.
2. File a written request for an immediate inspection whenever they fear imminent danger in their workplace.
3. Refuse in good faith to expose themselves to a hazardous condition—anything that a reasonable person would perceive as life-threatening or capable of causing serious injury.
4. Respond to questions from OSHA.
5. Review information in your files concerning job-related accidents and injuries.

It's always best to let your employees know about potential workplace hazards, including possible exposure to dangerous materials. In fact, several states have enacted laws requiring employers to inform their employees about workplace exposure to toxic substances. Also, the National Labor Relations Board has ruled that employers must supply union representatives with the names of chemicals and other toxic substances that might affect the union rank and file on the job.

As you might expect, you won't get far in court if you fire an employee for refusing to work under hazardous conditions. You might not realize, however, that "hazardous conditions" may include the people who work for you! An employee who uses drugs or alcohol can be considered a workplace hazard if he or she harms fellow employees or clients. I'll have a lot more to say about dealing with "toxic workers" in Chapter 4.

Injuries and Workers' Comp

An employee who gets injured on the job or who contracts an occupational disease such as black lung or asbestosis can receive financial support under state workers' compensation laws. These laws pay benefits to injured workers with a minimum of red tape and without the need to pin blame on anyone for the injury.

Most states require you to provide workers' comp protection for your employees. Penalties for not following the law can be pretty harsh.

Because each state has its own workers' comp law and operates its own system, the amount of compensation, duration of benefits, and procedures for making and settling claims vary widely. In general, however, an employee has a set amount of time to inform his or her employer of an occupational injury, and exceeding this time limit can derail the employee's claim.

Typical workers' comp benefits include medical payments for a period of disability or for permanent disability, rehabilitation services, death benefits, and burial expenses. Some states even award workers' compensation for disability caused by work-related stress—including stress related to alleged sexual discrimination.

The money for workers' comp payments may come from private insurance companies, state compensation funds, or employers' self-insurance programs. In the public sector, the Office of Workers' Compensation Programs, a branch of the Department of Labor, administers the Federal Employees Compensation Act, the Mine Safety and Health Act, and the Longshoremen's and Harbor Workers' Compensation Act.

Workers' compensation is bedrock law. Unless you want to put your company in scalding-hot water, don't ever fire an employee for filing a workers' comp claim or receiving benefits.

THE MONEY GAME

Some laws, particularly those involving pay, pensions, and so on, have become so ingrained in the American employment system that we tend to forget about them. Taking employment laws for granted, however, is rarely a good idea. These laws are an integral part of our work culture, and it's important to know how they function, even if they don't play a direct role in discipline and firing. After all, how can you know when you cross the line if you can't remember where the line is?

Minimum Wages and Overtime

Everyone receives a minimum wage, right? Guess again.

The Fair Labor Standards Act (FLSA) stipulates a minimum wage and overtime pay for *covered workers*. Although that's a broad category, it does not include executive, administrative, and professional employees; outside salespeople; workers in local retail or service establishments; and some agricultural workers.

Under the FLSA, most covered workers are entitled to one and one-half times their regular rate of pay for more than 40 hours of work per week. The law does not require premium overtime pay for covered agricultural workers, live-in household workers, taxicab drivers, and employees of motor carriers, railroads, and airlines. Employees of hospitals, nursing homes, and rest homes may receive overtime after 8 hours of work in a day or after 80 hours in a 14-day period.

The FLSA is enforced by the Wage and Hour Division of the Employment Standards Administration, a branch of the Department of Labor. When Wage and Hour compliance officers receive a complaint of an FLSA violation, they investigate to see if it's valid. The Wage and Hour Division always tries to persuade violators to comply with the law before referring the case to the Solicitor's Office of the Department of Labor, which may decide to file suit against the employer in federal court.

Under the FLSA, an employee also has the right to sue an employer for back pay, damages, attorney's fees, and court costs. If an employee begins a private suit, however, the Department of Labor won't pursue his or her case in court. To recover back pay, the employee must file the suit within two years for most violations, three years for intentional violations.

Unemployment

When workers are laid off (and sometimes when they quit or are terminated), they usually make a beeline for the unemployment office. But employees aren't the only ones who have to deal with unemployment. You also need to know how unemployment operates—your company is helping to pay for it.

Unemployment insurance is a benefit paid for a limited time to eligible workers when they are involuntarily unemployed. Its purpose is to tide unemployed workers over until they find jobs for which they are reasonably suited in terms of training, previous experience, and past wages. Claimants receive their cash benefits as a matter of right; benefits seldom cover all expenses, so need doesn't really enter the picture.

Unemployment insurance is a combined federal-state system: Federal law establishes minimum requirements, but each state administers its own program. State law determines who is eligible, how much money each person receives, and how long he or she can receive benefits. To be eligible in most programs, an unemployed person should not only be able to work, but should be actively seeking and available for suitable work.

Almost all workers are covered by unemployment insurance. Although each state specifies the amount of weekly and total payments and the manner in which they are calculated, the jobless worker usually receives about half of his or her former weekly wage. Most states limit the payment period to 26 weeks, but some continue to pay benefits for as long as 28 to 39 weeks. There's also a special program that extends payments for up to 13 additional weeks if claimants exhaust their benefits during times of high unemployment in the state.

Many states won't allow workers to receive unemployment if they quit their jobs for reasons that have nothing to do with the job or the employer. Other states disqualify workers who leave their jobs to get married, move to another area with a spouse, or take care of children. Some states, however, do pay benefits to workers who quit their jobs for compelling personal reasons; they make decisions about benefit payments on a case-by-case basis according to individual circumstances.

Wage Garnishment

People used to be hauled off to prison for failing to pay their bills. Fortunately, that's no longer the case. Debtors still have to pay up or enter bankruptcy, but they now have a legal safety net while they try to straighten out their finances.

During garnishment proceedings, debtors are protected by Title III of the Consumer Credit Protection Act, which is enforced by the Wage and Hour Division. This law limits the amount of disposable income that creditors can garnish and prevents workers from being fired because of garnishment for any single debt. Many states have garnishment laws that provide even more protection.

So, you may not love the idea of having a debtor on your staff, but you can't fire that employee merely because he or she has never learned how to balance a checkbook. Debtors have rights, too.

Pensions

With nearly 50 years at Frangible Enterprises, Bob V. is looking forward to his retirement—he's amassed a tidy little sum in the company pension fund. Imagine his surprise when he is let go right before his retirement date!

If Bob does a little digging, he might find that Frangible fired him to avoid paying him his pension. And that's a clearcut violation of the Employee Retirement Income Security Act (ERISA) of 1974.

The ERISA protects the interests of workers and their beneficiaries who depend on benefits from employee pension and welfare plans. The law establishes standards of conduct for trustees and administrators of welfare and pension plans, and requires plan administrators to disclose plan provisions and financial information. It also sets up funding, participation, and vesting requirements for pension plans, as well as an insurance system for certain benefit plans that terminate without having enough money to pay pensions to plan participants.

The Department of Labor and the Internal Revenue Service share responsibility for administering the ERISA. The Pension

Benefit Guaranty Corporation handles the pension plan termination insurance program.

Your right to fire, as we've seen again and again, is roped in by personnel laws. In this chapter, you've met the ones that you're most likely to bump into when you must discipline or fire employees. But don't stop here! Laws change all the time. Stay on top of the changes to stay out of the courtroom.

Even if you don't have the time or energy to master every termination-related law on the books, you'll be in good shape if you follow this simple guideline:

Never use race, age, sex, union activity, or other factors that have nothing to do with job performance as an excuse to fire or discipline employees.

CHAPTER 3

THE RIGHT WAY TO FIRE

Disciplining or firing employees can cause employers more trouble than they ever dreamed possible. It's all too easy to give an employee the axe for the wrong reason.

Consider the story of Randy D. and Louise J., a couple who worked for Foobaron International. They'd been dating for a year when Randy had to attend a business meeting in San Diego. Louise decided to surprise Randy by joining him the weekend after the meeting. She spent her own money for airline tickets and a hotel room in La Jolla. When Randy and Louise got back from their romantic interlude, a surprise was waiting for them: pink slips.

Randy and Louise were mystified. They'd both been doing good work, and Foobaron gave no reason for firing them. They soon learned the truth. Their weekend trip had offended their supervisor, a born-again Christian who did not approve of unmarried employees "shacking up" in hotel rooms. Randy and Louise wasted no time in suing the company for wrongful discharge and breach of contract.

During the trial, Foobaron's attorney argued that the employment-at-will doctrine gives employers the right to fire noncontract employees for any reason. But the judge didn't buy it. He held that the two employees had an implied contract with Foobaron that made it necessary for the company to justify their firing. Moreover, Foobaron had violated its own policies, because its employee manuals and personnel bulletins stated that employees could be fired only for "just cause." Randy and Louise collected a tidy sum from Foobaron in damages.

This cautionary tale neatly sums up why so many ex-employees are beating their former bosses in court. It's a prime example of the kind of Victorian thinking I warned you against earlier in this book.

Employers do not lose termination suits because the scales of justice are tipped unfairly in favor of employees. They lose because they fire or discipline employees in a way that raises judicial hackles.

Obviously, there's a wrong way to fire—but there's also a right way. You have to be careful, and you have to follow the rules. But you'll find that doing things properly is worth it in the long run.

THE RIGHT REASONS

Althea M. was fired from a senior managerial slot with a major accounting firm because she wasn't meek and mild enough to endear herself to the Old Boy network that comprised the firm's upper-level management. When she sued the firm for wrongful discharge on the basis of sex discrimination, she won easily. Along with $250,000 in damages, the firm had to pay $100,000 of Althea's legal fees. In this case, as in so many others, an organization made a fatal mistake about its termination rights: It thought it could do whatever it wished.

Employers are usually vulnerable in firing suits because of bad decisions such as this one, but poor documentation and faulty evaluation and termination policies are also to blame. To reduce your legal risks, you may have to revamp your organization's disciplinary and termination procedures as well as its reasons for firing.

Of course, there's a chance that you won't have to worry about any of these things. If you have a classic at-will employment relationship, you can fire an employee for any reason— good, bad, indifferent. You simply say, "You're fired," and it's a done deed.

These days, however, few employers have a classic at-will relationship with their employees. The courts have made so many exceptions to the at-will rule that the rule itself has almost become the exception. What's more, employers have developed rules of their own (and woe unto the employer who disregards them, as in the case of Randy and Louise). The upshot is that employers must have airtight reasons for disciplining or firing employees.

What does the law consider justifiable grounds for termination? The legally acceptable reasons aren't that different from many employers': poor performance, insubordination, criminal activity, and the like. The major caveat is that you cannot use good reasons for getting rid of problem employees to mask bad reasons, such as discriminating against members of minority groups or retaliating against whistle-blowers.

Poor Performance

You have every right in the world to fire an employee who does a bad job. Getting work done is, after all, the point of most organizations. Even written employment contracts state that the employment relationship will continue only as long as the employee's work is satisfactory.

You've probably heard the horror story about the employer who fired an African-American, a woman, or a disabled veteran for poor job performance and immediately got slapped with a discrimination suit. Like most oft-told tales, this one contains a few grains of truth. But it doesn't mean you should never fire an employee who belongs to a group protected by law.

For one thing, no judge is going to bother with a frivolous suit in which an employee is clearly using discrimination to get back at his or her former employee. Belonging to a protected group does not automatically immunize an employee against being disciplined or fired.

Sally K., a quadriplegic, claimed that Zyzz Corp. fired her from her programming job because providing special facilities for her was costing the company too much money. Zyzz countered that Sally's programs had brought the company's operations to a standstill on several occasions and that she consistently missed deadlines for crucial projects. Sally lost her suit against Zyzz, because all the evidence indicated that she really wasn't a very good programmer. Thus, the law lets you fire a member of a protected group if that person's work is not up to par.

Always document employees' poor performance. In termination cases, it doesn't hurt to show that you gave a problem employee a chance to improve lackluster performance, particularly if that employee worked for you for several years. Such documentation shows the court that you didn't use poor performance as an excuse to get rid of the employee.

Insubordination

Most courts view insubordination as a legitimate reason to fire an employee. Again, watch out when you terminate members of protected groups who flout your rules or authority; they may claim that you actually fired them because of their race, ethnic background, religion, sex, or disability. To counter such charges, you must be able to provide hard evidence that the employee was flagrantly disobedient.

You won't fare well in court, though, if the so-called insubordination boils down to the employee's refusal to break the law or do something that goes against the grain of public policy. An employee who bucks his or her boss's orders to bribe prospective clients or to work in an unsafe environment is *not* being insubordinate.

Absenteeism and Tardiness

The courts recognize that employers can't really run their businesses if employees consistently play hooky from work or show up an hour late every day. Even with judicial approval, however, dealing with employee absenteeism and tardiness is not as straightforward as it may seem.

When it comes to terminating for absenteeism, you have a procedural choice: You can distinguish between excused and unexcused absences, or you can treat all absences the same.

At first glance, you may think there's nothing peculiar about a policy that mandates different categories of employee absences. Many companies excuse employees from work to attend a family funeral, to serve on a jury, or even to go on a paid sabbatical. What many employers don't realize is that employees often charge employers with "subjective and arbitrary application" of excused absence policies in termination disputes.

The alternative is to dismiss employees after a certain number of absences, legitimate or not. But this type of policy creates more problems than it solves, because it can make an employer seem callous, biased, or unfair.

So, firing because of absenteeism alone is seldom a good idea. If absenteeism affects performance, however, that's another story. And don't feel too bad about firing an employee who thinks he or she should get a blue ribbon for showing up at work once in a while!

Legally, terminating for tardiness may be another hot potato. A judge may view overly strict tardiness policies as arbitrary and repressive, particularly if they single out members of a protected group. In other words, don't fire an employee because he or she is five minutes late to work.

Because employees must put in a certain number of hours to get their work done, however, they must arrive more or less on time. That's why a policy of firing employees for excessive or continual tardiness is legally acceptable. Just make sure that your employees know about the policy, and that chronic latecomers receive plenty of warning before they get the axe.

Company Rule Violations

One of your employees, Maria R., is writing the Great American Novel. She is composing this masterpiece on your computer system. One day she monopolizes the only laser printer in the house to prepare a copy of the 500-page manuscript for her agent, tying up the printer for several hours and preventing other employees from printing material actually related to their jobs.

You call Maria into your office, show her a passage in the employee handbook stating that employees cannot use company equipment for personal projects, and warn her that she will lose her job if she continues to write her book on company time. A week later, you catch Maria making photocopies of the manuscript on the company Xerox machine during working hours. You fire her immediately. Will the termination hold up in court?

You bet! You have every right to expect your employees to be dedicated to your company's best interests, and that includes setting individual concerns aside during work hours. No judge is going to give you a hard time for firing a worker who breaks your rules—unless, of course, the rules are illegal.

Security Breaches

"Security" means different things to different organizations. It can encompass everything from locking the door at night to displaying a badge to a guard on entering company premises to keeping trade secrets out of competitors' hands. The one thing virtually all companies agree on is that an employee who presents a security threat to co-workers or the organization should get the boot.

You can immediately fire any employee who doesn't comply with your security guidelines, especially if you have a federal contract or work in a regulated industry. Just make sure that there's a good reason for your security measures—insurance restrictions, government rulings, client protection, and so on.

Dishonesty

Honesty is one of those qualities that's preached more than it's practiced on the American business scene. Still, you shouldn't become cynical or resigned about keeping dishonest employees in your work force.

The courts agree that the last thing you need is a thief in your employee ranks. Fire a sticky-fingered worker for embezzling, a computer scam, or even stealing petty cash, and you'll have the blessing of almost any judge. Employees who steal from their employers are lawbreakers, and they can be punished by the law.

Always make sure you have solid evidence to tie an employee to a theft or fraud before taking action. Even strong suspicions are not good enough.

You hear through the grapevine that Henry Q., an accountant, has cooked up a scheme to siphon off company funds into a dummy bank account. You have no proof that such an account exists. Still, you figure you should get rid of a possible white-collar criminal and save a few pennies, so you fire Henry. He sues you for defamation because he can't get an accounting job at any other firm in the area. Even if Henry was stealing, your decision to fire him before all the facts were in was not smart.

Some subtle forms of employee dishonesty may hurt your organization more than obvious ones such as theft. For example, employees may fudge their résumés to make themselves appear better and brighter than they really are. The discrepancy between paper skills and actual ability becomes apparent only after the worker has been on the job for a while. If your paper tiger is in a high-echelon or sensitive position, you may have a major disaster on your hands. So, if you find that there's less to an employee's education, training, or experience than meets the eye, go ahead and fire that person straightaway. The law will probably back you up. In fact, fabricating credentials on a résumé is a criminal misdemeanor in New York and a few other states.

Many employers are trying to combat employee dishonesty by having employees sign a code of ethics. An employer can then discipline or fire an employee who doesn't live up to the code.

Criminal Activity

As we've seen, most judges tend to support a termination when an employee does something wrong in the workplace. But you can't assume that a judge will support the firing of an employee who commits a crime *outside* the workplace.

Take assault and battery. Some employees have ferocious tempers and enjoy picking fights, both at and away from work. Fighting at the office is definitely your concern. Because employers are liable for what their employees do to others, the law gives you the authority to ensure that employees don't do grievous bodily harm to their co-workers or members of the public. Thus, you can discipline or fire an employee for in-house fighting. But fighting outside the workplace is not your problem unless it affects productivity or performance.

If you think you might have to fire an employee because of criminal activity, ask yourself two key questions.

First, has the employee actually been *convicted* of a crime? Being investigated by the police or a government agency, or even arrested, is not the same as being convicted. Your attitude toward employees accused of committing crimes must mirror the guiding principle of American justice: Everyone is innocent until proven guilty.

However, you *can* suspend an employee accused of a crime or move that employee to a less conspicuous or sensitive position in your organization. For example, you could shift a programmer under investigation for hacking to a computer operator post with no access to code or privileged information. But don't fire the employee unless the investigation results in a conviction or a plea arrangement with the government.

Second, does the crime have any relationship to the employee's job? A judge probably wouldn't balk at the termination of an investment banker convicted of money laundering or a hospital orderly convicted of rape. The same judge might have a problem with the termination of a secretary convicted of driving while intoxicated—unless, of course, driving is part of the secretary's job description.

Employee legal problems may not result in criminal prosecution. It's much more likely that an employee will become embroiled in a civil suit; after all, more than half of all Americans get divorced every year, and millions more sue one another for various reasons. Again, what happens outside the workplace is the employee's business, not yours. You should resist the temptation to fire an employee for becoming involved in a messy divorce or a garnishment proceeding. If the employee's civil litigation doesn't affect company image or employee job performance, ignore it.

Health and Safety Threats

Patsy K. operates a forklift on one of your construction sites. Although she's good at the job, she has a tendency to toss back a few too many beers at lunch. One day she has a near-miss with a load of building materials. You have a heart-to-heart talk with Patsy and encourage her to go to Alcoholics Anonymous. Not long after this discussion, she gets drunk and almost runs over her supervisor. Can you fire her? Yes, because Patsy has shown that she is a genuine threat to the health and safety of her co-workers. (I'll have more to say about workplace drinking and drug use in Chapter 4.)

But what about Fred J., a salesperson who has positive test results for the human immunodeficiency virus (HIV)? He might eventually develop AIDS. Isn't he just as much of a health threat as Patsy?

A few years ago, when little was known about AIDS transmission, you might have been able to get away with firing Fred to protect clients and other workers from the disease. Now we know it is difficult to spread AIDS. The courts take a dim view of firing an HIV-infected employee, and as long as the employee feels able to work and presents no possibility of infecting others, the employer must let him or her work. In some instances, you may have to allow an employee with AIDS to take work home, to work flexible hours, or to telecommute, but you can't use the employee's condition as an excuse to fire him or her.

Some diseases do present a health threat to others. Proscribed illnesses vary from industry to industry; food handlers, for instance, cannot have typhoid or tuberculosis. Numerous federal and state regulations protect the public against communicable diseases passed on by sick or unclean workers. The law is definitely on your side if you discipline or fire such employees.

An employee's bad hygiene may be a health hazard, or it may only be distasteful to co-workers and customers. By societal standards, employees who don't bathe or wash their clothes regularly are offensive. Because the law doesn't condone workplace behavior that is objectionable to others, you have the right to ask such employees to clean up their acts. After a tactful discussion, you can discipline the employee if you don't see (or smell) improvement.

Dress Code Infractions

Some bosses wish they could force every employee to adopt the "dress for success" look. Others don't care as long as employee attire is clean and neat.

In businesses that require interaction with the public, there are usually standards for professional appearance. For instance, a medical supplies salesperson who wears a studded motorcyle jacket, ripped jeans, and three earrings in each ear probably won't convince too many doctors to buy his products. (The same outfit may be perfectly acceptable, however, for an arranger at a record company.) A bank teller who comes to work in an old sweatshirt and shorts may imply to customers that the bank is pretty casual about their money, too. Like it or not, an employee must dress appropriately for the job.

You must make exceptions for employees who dress in a certain way because of their religious or cultural beliefs, as long as their attire doesn't create problems for your company's image. For instance, you would get into trouble if you fired a Hasidic Jew for wearing side curls, a beard, and a yarmulke, especially if this employee worked the night shift and never came into contact with the public.

THE RIGHT EVIDENCE

Having a good reason to fire an employee is not enough. You need proof of poor performance or bad behavior.

In court, you must be able to show that you investigated before you fired, especially in situations involving criminal activity or serious infractions of company policy. You don't have to prove the employee's wrongdoing beyond the shadow of a doubt; the law doesn't ask you to be a prosecuting attorney. It does ask you to demonstrate that you acted rationally and in good faith, and that you didn't jump to any conclusions before taking action.

Investigative Strategies

When they investigate in-house wrongdoing, employers in the private sector aren't always bound by the same constitutional constraints as employers in the public sector. For instance, the Bill of Rights prohibitions against unreasonable search and seizure (the Fourth Amendment) and self-incrimination (the notorious Fifth Amendment) don't apply to private employers.

This doesn't mean you should treat an in-house investigation as if you were running the Spanish Inquisition. Remember, the Constitution isn't the only law that governs employment. A heavy-handed investigation might violate state constitutional provisions; tort theories of negligence, outrageous conduct, or invasion of privacy; or statutory restrictions against, for example, polygraph testing of employees.

The safest way to investigate workplace infractions or crimes is to interview everyone involved, including possible witnesses. In some employee investigations, however, you can legally search lockers, desks, or filing cabinets, or use monitoring devices such as surveillance cameras or telephone taps. When you must investigate extremely serious crimes, forget about playing Sherlock Holmes—call the police or another outside agency.

Interview Techniques

Your job as an interviewer is to obtain facts and resolve contradictions. All the law requires is that you give an interview your best shot; if employees or witnesses aren't willing to cooperate, that's not your problem. Being overly zealous about questioning employees *is* your problem: You may cross the line from legitimate inquiry to illegal coercion. In employee investigations, you don't win by intimidation. Threats might get you a few more answers, but more likely they'll get you sued.

Searches

Many employers don't realize that they have the right to conduct searches if they're reasonably sure that a crime has been committed. For instance, you can look for stolen property in an employee's desk, filing cabinets, locker, lunchbox, toolbox, purse, or clothing (see Table 3–1). You can also conduct a search if you suspect on-the-job drug use or dealing, as I'll explain in the next chapter. And if a female employee accuses male coworkers of sexual harassment, a search of desks or lockers might turn up sexually offensive material that validates her claims.

Before you do any kind of search, however, *obtain consent*. Never use force in searching employees or their property. You

TABLE 3–1
Guidelines for Employee Searches

Avoid unauthorized searches of employees and their property, including their automobiles.

Search employees only if you have good reason to believe that they're in possession of stolen or prohibited materials at the time of the search.

Before you search, try to obtain the strongest possible evidence that an employee has taken company property or is holding contraband. For instance, a reliable worker may tell a supervisor that he or she saw the suspect stealing the property. Or you may actually smell alcohol on the suspect's breath.

Whenever possible, discuss your suspicions with the employee you think is holding stolen company property or prohibited materials. Don't draw attention to the discussion or let other employees overhear it. An employee who is obviously nervous or who gives farfetched answers to your questions may well be guilty.

Always exercise good judgment and common sense. If you're not sure whether to search, talk to other managers and the legal department.

You can take stolen property or prohibited material from an employee if it is in "plain view"—the stolen screwdriver is sticking out of the employee's pocket, or the cocaine vial is sitting on the employee's desk. If the stolen goods or prohibited materials are not in plain view, you can search the employee's person and/or immediate personal effects, but only if the employee gives you permission.

You don't need permission to search lockers, toolboxes, containers, or storage areas that you have supplied for work-related use by employees. You should, however, give employees the opportunity to open their own lockers, toolboxes, and so on. Do not search wallets, purses, or lunchboxes in work-related containers or storage areas without obtaining permission from their owners.

Avoid unnecessary embarrassment to employees. For example, only a woman should conduct an authorized physical search of female employees.

---

can tell employees that if they balk at the search, you may have to assume that they have something to hide. Under current law, you can also tell employees who don't agree to legitimate searches that they may be disciplined or sent home. But the law definitely does not permit you to threaten employees with termination if they don't permit you to search them or their property.

Be sure to spread the word to employees about your search policies. It's a good idea to post notices by the main entrance of all buildings, and in employee locker rooms and common areas (see Table 3–2).

TABLE 3–2
Sample Search Notices

General Notice of Search Policy

Notice: To prevent theft of company or employee property, or use or possession of drugs or alcohol, all bags, purses, lunchboxes, and parcels are subject to inspection whenever an employee enters or leaves the premises.

Notice of Locker Room Search Policy

Notice: The company provides lockers for the use of its employees during work hours. Each locker has a combination lock that can be opened with the company's master key. No other lock may be placed on the locker. The company reserves the right to open and inspect the interior of each locker at any time.

Prohibited items, including nonprescription illegal drugs, alcohol, or weapons, may not be placed in the lockers. Lockers will be maintained in a neat and sanitary condition. The company is not responsible for articles that are lost or stolen from the lockers.

Surveillance and Monitoring

Be very careful about which surveillance techniques you use to establish your case. The surveillance you think is so necessary may be intrusive under state statutes or the common law.

You hear that Jane P. is selling drugs to other female employees, so you instruct your security personnel to install a video camera in the women's locker room. The security guard spends a great deal of time scanning the locker room; oddly, he comes up with no evidence that Jane or anyone else is dealing drugs. It doesn't take long for the female employees to band together and lodge a sexual harassment complaint against the guard and your company. Clearly, it's worth finding out whether a mode of surveillance is legitimate before you invest time, technology, and trouble!

So far, there's no federal law against telephone monitoring. Companies often monitor operators to check on the number of calls they handle per minute and whether they are courteous to customers.

Under certain conditions, you may use telephone monitoring for in-house investigations. Let's assume that you're sadder but wiser after your experience with video surveillance. You now have a line on another possible employee drug dealer, Mark L. You gather your evidence by monitoring Mark's sales calls— something that your company does anyway. This time, you hit pay dirt: Mark is not only dealing cocaine from work, but also promising it to clients for buying your company's products. You give Mark a warning and ask him to enter a drug rehabilitation program.

Again, you must tread cautiously, because the law does regulate telephonic eavesdropping. In some states, telephone monitoring is forbidden unless the subject consents to it or unless the monitoring is part of day-to-day business operations. Check local laws before you monitor employee telephone calls for any reason.

Unions and Investigations

Investigating employees who belong to a union with which you have a collective bargaining agreement is sometimes tricky. The main thing to remember is that a union representative can be present during an interview with a union employee, if that's what the employee wants. Denying an employee's request for union representation is an unfair labor practice.

On the other hand, you don't have to call in the union every time you wish to question one of its members. You should be able to obtain the information you need without ruffling union feathers if you keep in mind that:

1. You don't have to provide union representation unless an employee asks for it.
2. An employee cannot ask for a union representative unless the employee believes that he or she will be disciplined as a result of the investigation's findings.
3. The union representative cannot stand in the way of your legitimate goals.
4. You do not have to bargain with the representative. You can even insist that he or she remain silent during the interview.

THE RIGHT RECORDS

Whenever you must discipline or fire an employee, write down *everything* connected with the matter, no matter how trivial it may seem. If you're on the receiving end of a wrongful discharge suit, it helps to have a record of the employee's deficiencies, the warnings given to him or her, and the disciplinary action taken. You don't have to write a book; a brief summary of the facts will usually suffice. Local, state, and federal laws can tell you how much to record and how to store the information.

Many states have passed laws that give employees the right to see and respond to material in their personnel or medical files. Faced with such laws, employers may have to walk a fine line between keeping enough documentation on hand to satisfy the courts and culling out material that could be disastrous if it fell into employee hands.

In general, though, you'll be on solid ground if your records show that:

1. You told the employee what was expected of him or her.
2. You warned the employee to improve performance or alter behavior within a certain time frame.
3. The poor performance or improper behavior continued after you gave the employee a chance to improve.

Fair Warning

The all-important first step is to let problem employees know exactly why they are being disciplined or fired. This "notice" can be verbal or written. It probably makes the most sense to back up a verbal warning with a written memo.

Giving notice may take all your diplomatic and communication skills. If your reasons for dismissing an employee are vague and overly general ("I don't like the way you do things"), the firing will probably go right out the courtroom window. The judge may find that your grounds for termination were too subjective, or that you didn't really give the employee a proper idea of the performance or behavior you expected.

But overly detailed reasons for firing can hang you, too. Given too much to work with, an arbitrator or judge will probably be able to find something that puts your company in the hot seat. Obviously, there are advantages and drawbacks to both approaches; what you decide to do may change from situation to situation.

The Well-Laid Paper Trail

Records can make or break a wrongful discharge case. Don't let a defense attorney punch holes in your records!

To get the judge, jury, or hearing officer on your side, you usually must provide documentary evidence in the form of personnel records, application forms, memos, notes, and so on. You may also have to produce witnesses to give verbal testimony—their version of what happened.

In an arbitration hearing or trial, proof boils down to who seems more believable. Here are some guidelines for developing documentary evidence that will enhance your credibility.

Keep Comprehensive Records. Employee personnel files are often the main source of evidence in a termination case. Make sure yours contain the right information. Each worker file should include a detailed employee history with records of all warnings, notices, disciplinary actions, counseling sessions, suspensions, and complaints from supervisors, co-workers, customers, or members of the public.

If your records show that an employee has missed at least 15 days of work per month for the past two years, the court may agree that you had an excellent reason to dismiss that employee. Thorough records can also defuse sexual harassment and discrimination suits. If a salesperson alleges that she was fired because of her sex, her claim won't carry much weight if the files state that she consistently failed to meet sales quotas and that several clients complained about her unscrupulous business practices.

Every time you warn an employee about improper on-the-job behavior or poor performance, put a note in his or her file. Documentary evidence of warnings issued over a period of weeks, months, or even years can undercut an employee's claim that you used poor performance as a cover-up for discriminatory termination policies. There's no such thing as too little documentation!

How do you find out what kind of job an employee is doing? From employee evaluations, of course. Many employers use evaluations as the basis for issuing warnings or even for firing employees. It's not surprising that evaluations eventually become crucial documentary evidence for employers and employees alike.

An evaluation will not help your case unless it lists employee shortcomings as well as achievements. Make sure, however, that supervisors don't get *too* negative in their evaluation comments. Although judges rarely hold employers liable for making mistakes about employee performance, a judge might perceive unconstructive criticism as evidence of malice or "reckless disregard" for the truth of the information. The key, then, is a temperate evaluation that honestly appraises an employee's work.

Segregate Personnel Files.　As a requirement for federal or state laws or an affirmative action program, you may have to compile potentially inflammatory data on the age, sex, race, ethnic group, national origin, and marital status of your employees. Keeping this information in a separate location from personnel files ensures employee privacy and avoids the appearance of discrimination.

Fix Incorrect Information.　The law recognizes that employers are human and sometimes misjudge their employees.

Sue H. is Mary N.'s supervisor. Sue thinks Mary has been padding her travel expense reports. Despite Mary's protests that the expense reports are legit, Sue puts a note in Mary's file that Mary is untrustworthy and shouldn't be allowed to go on company trips. Later it turns out that Sue has misplaced receipts that validate all of Mary's reported expenses.

What should Sue do now? If she's smart, she'll correct Mary's file immediately. Better yet, she'll remove the incriminating comments from the file.

Even though the law lets you err once in a while, it also demands that you correct your mistakes. So, if an employee accused of a crime or rule violation is vindicated, ensure that his or her file is updated right away.

Maintain Backup Files.   You never know when files will be destroyed or stolen, so it doesn't hurt to set up backup employee records. You can keep backups on a computer or make photocopies of the original records. Whatever you do, store the backup records in a separate location than the originals—in another building or on a different computer system.

Needless to say, the purpose of a backup personnel file system is *not* to provide a repository for material that you don't want employees to see. In other words, don't try to hide derogatory correspondence or incriminating photographs in the backup records.

THE RIGHT OPTIONS

After you've gathered and documented your evidence, the next step is to fire that problem employee . . . right?

Not always. You have the right to fire an employee for serious infractions of your rules. But firing may not be your only choice. It's safer to consider other options when the evidence isn't ironclad, or when your hands aren't entirely clean and it's fairly certain that the firing will prompt a lawsuit.

Let Problem Employees Resign.   Asking an employee to quit instead of firing him or her outright may seem like a good idea; both sides save face. In such cases, the employer requests the employee to sign a release that permits him or her to get out gracefully.

One small glitch is that an employee who resigns under such circumstances may as well have been fired as far as unemployment offices, unions, state fair employment offices, and the Equal Employment Opportunity Commission are concerned. Although a voluntary resignation and release may be enough to insulate you from immediate posttermination problems, they won't do you much good if the "firing" comes back to haunt you later.

Moreover, allowing an employee to resign instead of being fired might be taking on some undesirable legal baggage. The resignation agreement, for instance, may demand that you not tell others the real reason for the employee's departure from your ranks, or that you purge the employee's personnel files. If you think these terms are loaded, you're right.

Offering to get rid of an employee's records in exchange for a release can be deadly if the employee decides to sue you for wrongful discharge—you won't have the vital documentation you need for your defense. To avoid such problems, sanitize but don't completely destroy the records. Retain a skeleton file with only the dates the employee worked for you, a description of the position or classification the employee held, and his or her starting and ending salary figures.

Let Problem Employees Transfer. Transferring an employee to another department or company location sometimes makes more sense than firing him or her. In cases of poor performance and excessive absenteeism, appropriate supervision or a change of scene might take care of the problem. Of course, a transfer is not a reasonable solution if the employee is a thief or drug dealer, or if he or she constantly fights with co-workers.

Why consider a transfer? Because, as you know well, hiring and training employees costs money.

Tom D. has been a teller with your bank for many years. Because he has done a superior job, you decide that he deserves a promotion to customer service representative. Unfortunately, Tom turns out to be an abysmal customer service rep; he loses loan papers, he gets flustered by the simplest customer demands, he's obviously not happy. Now, you don't want to lose an experienced employee, but you also don't want to ruin the bank's image by having someone in a highly visible position who can't handle the job.

Your solution is not to fire Tom, despite his poor performance, but to offer him a transfer to another branch, where he'll supervise and train the teller staff. He accepts with alacrity. This compromise lets you take advantage of Tom's experience in a way that benefits both him and the bank. And, as a side benefit, you bypass some nasty litigation.

Give Problem Employees One Last Chance. No one can sell your company's auto parts like Gerald M. He's won countless bonuses and sales awards, and is well liked by both staff and customers. He's also been with the company for 30 years.

Recently, however, you learned that Gerry made a large number of personal calls on the company WATS line and that he allowed his son to come into the office during work hours and use the company computer and printer to write a college term paper. You like Gerry and want to keep him on staff, but you can't allow him to continue abusing company resources. What should you do?

You do need to impose some kind of discipline. Putting Gerry on probation or suspending him from work without pay for a certain period might teach him the right kind of lesson. Also, you don't want to run the risk of one employee who commits an offense receiving substantially different treatment from another who commits the same offense. That's a sure way to get yourself sued for discrimination.

Probation and suspension are less damaging to employee morale than firing. These options also mean that you don't have to sacrifice a valued employee to show the rest of the work force what will happen if they break your rules.

Use probation and suspension only to deal with problems that an employee can correct within the time frame of the probation. And don't keep putting an incorrigible employee on probation as an alternative to firing him or her. The goal of probation and suspension is that employees learn from their mistakes—when an employee can't or won't improve, probation and suspension are just ways of staving off the inevitable. Moreover, continual probation may dampen the morale of other employees. Probation, after all, is an attention getter.

Doing things right is no guarantee that you'll never be the target of a wrongful discharge suit or government investigation. Still, you'll go a long way to protect yourself if you remember this:

Fire employees only for good reasons. Follow your own rules, and be fair.

CHAPTER 4

POISON IN THE WORKPLACE

Some people like to think that cocaine and "crack" are problems only for teenage gang members in urban ghettoes. Others believe that you're not an alcoholic unless you look like a reject from the state mental hospital and smell like a distillery. Every day, countless American workers, in all jobs, at all income levels, from all walks of life, prove these myths wrong.

As an employer, your concern is what to do about workers who drink or use drugs on the job. These days, you can't simply find out who the workplace substance abusers are, fire them, and have that be the end of the story.

Arthur J., a widget salesperson for Smedley, Inc., had a drinking problem. Some days he felt so lousy that he didn't go to work. Unfortunately, those days began to add up.

Art's boss fired him after he missed nine months of work in four years. Art won a job discrimination suit, however, when he charged Smedley with violating the Federal Rehabilitation Act of 1973. A U.S. District Court judge declared that Art was "legally crippled" by alcoholism and that his boss should have helped him get counseling before letting him go. The judge also ruled that because Art had voluntarily dried out and was faithfully attending Alcoholics Anonymous, he should be allowed to reapply for his old job. The judge also ordered Smedley to give Art more than $150,000 in back pay.

The process of identifying workplace drunks and druggies is a legal mine field. Every jurist seems to have a different opinion on the matter. But that's not all you need to worry about.

One Oregon judge, for instance, recently ruled that positive results of a urinalysis test for marijuana use, among other things, were not enough to keep a worker from receiving unemployment benefits—or even to get that worker fired in the first place. Urinalysis can show that someone used marijuana within about 30 days of testing, the judge noted, but the test does not tell exactly when the drug was ingested or whether it impaired the employee's on-the-job performance.

The issue, then, is not whether an employee has an occasional joint after work, but whether he or she is smoking, snorting, or sipping at work. Regrettably, that's exactly what many employees *are* doing.

The American workplace has become a free port for drug abuse, possesion, and sale. All too often, employees steal to finance their drug habits. Company property becomes the "currency" that makes employee drug abuse possible.

The rise of workplace drug abuse does not mean that workplace alcohol abuse has stopped. Drinking on the job continues to be a serious, unresolved problem.

Employees who work under the influence of drugs or alcohol represent a grave safety hazard to themselves, their co-workers, and the public. If their behavior is not curbed or at least challenged, substance-abusing employees can destroy a business. Theft and safety issues aside, employees who are impaired by drugs or alcohol are unproductive, error-prone, and unreliable.

Some employers give up the battle against workplace substance abuse because they think they don't have enough legal ammunition. Well, they're wrong. You *can* act decisively to rid your workplace of substance abuse without getting into trouble with the law.

I'll be the first to admit that the legal road to a substance-free workplace has its share of potholes and hairpin turns. Still, it's better to follow that road than to bulldoze your way with a substance abuse policy that tramples on employee rights and involves you in an endless round of litigation. Getting sued is no way to deal with workplace drug and alcohol abuse!

THE LATEST LAWS

A fortunate development for employers is that Congress has staked out the workplace as a major front in the War on Drugs. Over the last few years, Congress has passed several important pieces of legislation that should assist you in fighting the good fight against employee substance abuse. Remember, though, that even the most helpful laws can bite you if you don't follow them.

Anti-Drug Abuse Act of 1986

This act stiffens penalties for all federal drug-related offenses and also provides funds to federal, state, and local agencies for strengthening prevention, education, treatment, and law enforcement programs.

The new, tough penalties, which apply to employees who abuse drugs, include:

1. Prison terms ranging from 10 years to life, with no possibility of probation or parole, for offenses involving drug dealing.
2. Fines of up to $5 million and prison terms of up to 40 years for offenses involving 500 grams of cocaine or crack or 100 grams of heroin.
3. A fine of up to $1,000 for a first offense involving simple possession of a controlled substance, up to $2,500 for a second offense, and at least $5,000 plus 90 days in jail for all subsequent offenses.

The Anti-Drug Abuse Act differs from past legislation in that it specifically targets users as well as dealers. It also calls for synthetic drugs to be treated as controlled substances for law enforcement purposes.

This act is a double-edged sword for employers—it gives them some heavy artillery to deploy against workplace drug abusers, but also forces them to shoulder some heavy legal burdens.

These days, you may get socked with criminal penalties if you tolerate the presence of drug users, sellers, or distributors in your organization. What's more, the act may encourage workers and others who are harmed by drug-abusing employees in your organization to shift the blame to you for keeping those employees on your payroll.

Drug-Free Workplace Act

If you have a federal contract for $25,000 or more, you must now certify that you will make a good-faith effort to keep your organization free of drugs. The act stipulates that you must do the following:

1. Notify employees in writing that the manufacture, distribution, possession, or use of controlled substances is prohibited in the workplace.
2. Describe the punitive action that you will take if employees make, use, or sell drugs in the workplace.
3. Tell employees that as a condition of employment with your organization, they must abstain from drugs, and must also let you know if they are convicted for workplace substance abuse.
4. Require employees convicted of workplace substance abuse violations to participate in a treatment or rehabilitation program.

If an employee does inform you that he or she has been convicted of violating a law against workplace substance abuse, you must take action within 30 days. This action can range from telling convicted abusers to enter approved drug rehabilitation programs to firing them if they refuse to undergo treatment.

Here's what the act asks you to do if your contract was issued after March 18, 1989:

1. Notify employees in writing that the manufacture, distribution, possession, or use of controlled substances is prohibited in the workplace.

2. Set up a program to inform employees about the dangers of drug abuse in the workplace and the availability of employee assistance programs.
3. Make a good-faith effort to continue to keep your organization free of drugs.

If you fail to do these things, the federal government may suspend your payments or contract; it may even take you out of the running for future contract consideration. The government will look at several factors to determine whether you're living up to your pledge to maintain a drug-free workplace, but the number of employees convicted of workplace drug offenses is probably the most critical.

WHOSE PROBLEM IS IT, ANYWAY?

The courts, like Congress, understand that employee substance abuse is a serious problem. In an effort to contain the tidal wave of drug and alcohol abuse in the workplace, many judges are giving employers considerable latitude in disciplining and firing abusers.

The courts do not merely grant employers the power to discipline abusers; they expect employers to take a stand against workplace substance abuse. That's because the courts hold employers accountable for losses or injuries that innocent third parties suffer because of substance-abusing employees, especially if the employer knows that the employee has a problem with drugs or alcohol. Careful, though! Overly aggressive action against on-the-job drug use and drinking also falls outside the legal pale.

Recently, the courts have added even more spice to this stew by asking employers to offer assistance to substance-abusing employees before they get to the point of harming others. Failing to help (or halt) such employees can mean harsh criminal penalties.

So, dealing with employee substance abuse means walking a fine line between doing nothing and doing too much. Tricky, yes . . . but definitely doable.

Better Safe Than Sorry

It's a well-established principle of law that employees have a right to work in a safe environment. The other side of the coin is that employers have an obligation to provide a work area that is free of unsafe conditions.

The courts have taken the position that an employee who is addicted to drugs or alcohol is as much of a safety hazard as a toxic chemical or defective machine. And it's up to the employer to remove all hazards from the workplace.

Because the courts believe that protecting the safety of workers is so important, they allow employees to sue an employer who fails to police the workplace properly. The government uses federal laws such as the Occupational Safety and Health Act to prosecute employers who look the other way when "hazardous" employees threaten the safety of their co-workers.

Employer responsibility for the safety of others doesn't end when a substance-abusing employee leaves work.

Gary D. smokes marijuana and takes his fourth Valium tablet of the day before leaving work at QED Circuit Boards. On the way home, he has a car crash in which several people are badly injured. Although the accident did not occur at the circuit board factory, QED may still face charges. Basically, the employer is in the same position as a host who doesn't prevent an obviously intoxicated guest from driving; if the guest gets into trouble on the road, the host may be legally liable.

Performance Is the Key

In general, the courts sympathize with employers who try to clean up substance abuse in the workplace. Before an employer can fire an employee for drug or alcohol abuse, however, an employer must demonstrate a link between the employee's abuse and his or her job performance. For instance, few judges would dispute the firing of a commercial airline pilot involved in a drug-related accident. Flying a jumbo jet demands both technical competence and the ability to win the confidence of the flying public.

But the courts won't rush to support the firing of a substance abuser if an employer can't prove a cause-and-effect relationship between abuse and performance.

HyCon Software fired Marcia N., a documentation writer, for pleading guilty to possession of marijuana; she sued to get her job back. Initially, the judge ordered HyCon to reinstate her because there was no demonstrable link between her marijuana use and the quality of the documentation she produced. As the suit developed, however, HyCon showed that Marcia's documentation was not as high-grade as it seemed. Several customers had complained that her latest doc set was obscure and difficult to use; others had pointed out errors and omissions. HyCon's corporate executives were not pleased. It was clear, said the judge, that Marcia's substance abuse had damaged the company's reputation for public service and integrity and had eroded the confidence of upper-level management. He upheld her termination.

So, the courts do allow (and sometimes encourage) you to discipline or fire substance abusers. But the firing or disciplinary action must be fair, nonabusive, and in tune with public interests. As always, you must discipline or fire for the right reasons and within the scope of existing law.

Check It Out

An employer who hires or retains an employee with a known history of substance abuse may be legally liable under the *negligent hiring* doctrine. This doctrine, recognized by most courts, demands that employers be careful about whom they hire and keep on staff.

Hiring or retaining a known sustance abuser could mean a lawsuit on the grounds that you didn't live up to your obligations as a manager. Your legal duty is to check out prospective or current employees who behave erratically. The courts see failure to do this screening as a breach of management responsibility.

Here's how to avoid being hit with a negligent hiring suit:

1. Make sure your company has a written policy that forbids the use of drugs or alcohol on the job.
2. Tell all prospective employees about the policy.

3. Train supervisors to recognize the warning signs of substance abuse (see Table 4–1).
4. Work with a qualified service provider to establish an employee assistance program for assisting employees with drug or alcohol problems (see Table 4–2).

TABLE 4–1
Signs of Employee Drug Abuse

Deterioration of personal appearance
Lack of inhibition
Droopy eyelids
Impaired vision
Constricted pupils
Decreased physical activity
Impaired coordination
Sweating, tremors, and restlessness
Constantly red or runny nose
Deteriorating job performance

TABLE 4–2
Model for Contract between Employer and Employee Assistance Program Provider

Recital

Brief description of basic elements of employer's program, employee assistance program (EAP) provider's independent contractor status, and services to be provided.

Detail of Services to Be Provided

EAP will diagnose and evaluate drug and alcohol abuse.
EAP will refer employees to detoxification programs as necessary.
EAP will provide counseling and/or treatment.
Employee will pay for a certain number of counseling or treatment sessions, as specified in the contract.

Provider Qualifications

All clinicians performing services for the EAP must be licensed.
Clinicians include clinical psychologists, psychiatrists, and social workers.
Clinicians must meet certain academic, internship, and experience requirements, as outlined in the contract.
Employer can review any outside service to which the EAP provider refers employees.

TABLE 4–2 *(concluded)*

Records

EAP provider must maintain records of all services for a specified period.
Employer has the right to audit the EAP provider's records to evaluate the
program, treatment results, and referral data.
EAP provider must give employer periodic activity or status reports.

Confidentiality

EAP provider must follow state and federal laws regarding the confidentiality
of employee records.

Indemnification

EAP provider should carry sufficient professional and public liability
insurance.
EAP provider should protect (indemnify) employer from injuries or damages
caused by EAP staff or employees.

Conditions for Termination of Contract

The employer can terminate the agreement without cause after a specified
warning period (notice), as given in the contract.
The employer can terminate the agreement without notice if either party
becomes insolvent or bankrupt, or if the provider fails to perform contracted
services.
The EAP provider must continue to meet indemnification and confidentiality
requirements after the agreement expires or is terminated.

TESTING, TESTING

Substance abuse testing has always trailed controversy in its
wake. Advocates of testing say that it is the only reasonable way
to cull out potentially dangerous abusers. Opponents point out
that testing violates basic privacy rights.

It's true that implementing an aggressive testing policy can
be risky. Under numerous federal and state laws, employers are
liable for ill-conceived or poorly run employee drug testing programs. This means that you must understand the legalities of
testing before you set up a testing program for your organization.

Testing Ways and Means

There are many different drug and alcohol screening techniques. The one you choose depends on your company's policies and pocketbook.

Nearly all drug testing programs use urinalysis to screen for drug metabolites, the chemical by-products formed and excreted after a drug is metabolized by the body's enzymes. At present, the two most commonly used urinalysis tests are enzyme immunoassay and radioimmunoassay. Enzyme immunoassay is a fast, inexpensive way to test for a variety of drugs and their by-products. Even personnel with minimal technical training can perform enzyme immunoassay tests.

But all immunoassay tests have a big drawback: unreliability. Although manufacturers claim accuracy rates as high as 99 percent, experts tend to agree that immunoassay testing cannot prove absolutely that a sample contains a particular drug or its metabolite. It's not surprising, then, that most courts reject immunoassay results that are not confirmed by other tests.

On and off the job, blood and breath tests are used to determine alcohol abuse. Blood tests for blood alcohol levels obtain the most accurate results, but many employers don't use them because they are expensive and time-consuming and because they must be administered by trained medical personnel. Also, blood tests are invasive. From a legal standpoint, they violate individual privacy rights (I'll explore privacy issues later in this chapter). Many employers opt to use Breathalyzers to test for alcohol abuse. When administered properly, the Breathalyzer exam offers a quick, cheap, and accurate way to determine an employee's actual blood alcohol level at the time of the test.

Blood alcohol and Breathalyzer tests provide evidence of impairment at the time of the test. Urinalysis assays, however, demonstrate only the presence of particular metabolites in an employee's urine; they don't prove conclusively that an employee is under the influence of a drug. For example, metabolites of THC, the psychoactive element in marijuana, often appear in urine three weeks after use—long after the intoxicating effects of the drug have worn off (see Table 4–3).

TABLE 4–3
Urinalysis Detection Time after Ingestion of Common Drugs

Drug(s)	Detection Time
Amphetamines	2 days
Barbiturates	1–21 days
Bendodiazepines (Valium, tranquilizers)	3 days
Cocaine	4 days
Methadone	3 days
Opiates	2 days
Cannabinoids (marijuana)	20 days
Methaqualone (Quaalude)	14 days

The upshot is that it's easier to use testing to gain evidence of workplace boozing than of workplace drug abuse. No drug test can prove beyond a shadow of a doubt that an employee has violated a policy against on-the-job substance abuse or is under the influence of a drug during work hours.

Therefore, some employers prefer to use less sophisticated—but just as effective—means of identifying employee drug abuse:

1. Searching lockers, desks, and other employee areas.
2. Using video cameras and other types of electronic surveillance.
3. Alerting security personnel to watch for signs of drug abuse.
4. Using specially trained "sniffer" dogs to locate hidden drugs, often on evenings and weekends when employees aren't around.

Searches and surveillance, as we've seen, are legal—as long as you don't go overboard in applying them.

Confirmation Testing

If a positive drug or alcohol test means that an employee will be disciplined or fired, *get a second opinion.* The ambiguous results of drug tests have come back to haunt many employers in court.

At present, one of the most accurate means of confirming urinalysis results is gas chromatography/mass spectrometry (GC/MS). A highly sophisticated process, GC/MS uses an electron beam to fragment a urine sample and isolate specific molecular structures found only in the drug or drugs in question.

GC/MS can verify the results of a positive urinalysis by providing strong scientific evidence that a suspected drug metabolite is present in a sample. Only trained specialists at a high-quality laboratory can properly perform GC/MS testing, so confirming positive urinalysis results can be quite expensive. Would you rather spend the money on a confirmation test or a court case?

Independent corroboration of urinalysis results, whether by GC/MS or any other method, can save your neck when you may have to discipline or terminate employees because of substance abuse. Even if an employee with a positive urine test admits that he or she has used drugs on the job, that's *not* confirmation of the urinalysis results. In fact, a clever attorney might make it appear that you somehow badgered the employee into confessing. Not even the cleverest attorney, however, can argue with a mass spectrometer.

MAKE TESTING WORK FOR YOU

If your testing program is to be a success, your employees must believe that it is a reliable means of detecting substance abuse. No employee is going to put much stock in an unreliable program that consistently turns up false-positive results. So, you must ensure utmost care in the way specimens are collected, labeled, transported, and maintained.

For urinalysis testing, the first step is to obtain a valid specimen from each employee. Direct observation of the employee during the collection process cuts down on opportunities for fraud and helps you establish an accurate "chain of custody" over each sample. But such observation is also very intrusive and embarrassing, so stay away from it unless you're fairly sure an employee is switching samples on you. Because of potential judicial hostility to observation, you might want to consider an alternative such as postcollection temperature monitoring, or not announcing the date and time of the test in advance.

Once you obtain the urine samples, make sure they're properly sealed, labeled, and numbered. Identifying information, including the employee's name, the name of the observer (if any), the sample number, and the time and date of collection, should be recorded for each sample in a ledger. This ledger should also give the time and date when each sample went to the laboratory for analysis, the time and date of its return, and the test results.

Establishing a documented chain of custody for the samples is critical. It may be the only way to prove that a sample actually belongs to the employee whose name appears on it. Therefore, the chain-of-custody document should identify everyone who handled the sample, as well as the time and date that the sample was transferred from person to person.

In drug testing, as in so many other things, nothing is over until it's over. Because a positive drug test can result in discipline or termination (and possibly a lawsuit, too), you need to build some legal fail-safe mechanisms into your testing program. Probably the easiest thing to do is to freeze and hang on to positive specimens after testing. Another fail-safe (remember, it never hurts to get a second opinion) is to allow employees to be retested by another laboratory.

Whether positive or negative, test results are confidential and should not be disseminated except on a need-to-know basis. If you tell half the company about an employee's positive drug test, you'll probably end up telling it to the judge, too.

When Should You Test?

Legally, you can test whenever you want to. On the other hand, you want to avoid the perception that you're testing out of the blue and for no good reason. Once you decide to implement a substance abuse testing program, it doesn't hurt to work out a policy on when and why the testing will be done.

Random testing can give you a lot of data on the extent of drug use in your work force. Many employers believe that random testing also deters employee substance abuse. The downside of random testing is that it can dampen employee morale and make your workers think you don't trust them. As you know, employee resentment can result in high turnover and reduced productivity.

Some employers ask employees to undergo *periodic testing* when they have their annual medical examinations. Other employers routinely test for drugs when employees move to more sensitive positions in the company. Employees always know about periodic tests in advance. The disadvantage of periodic tests, of course, is that substance-abusing employees usually have enough time to purge themselves of drugs and come out with squeaky-clean test results.

You can ask an employee to undergo *testing for cause* if circumstances lead you to believe that he or she is drunk or stoned. "Cause" might be a supervisor's observation that an employee looks or acts strange, comments from other staffers that the employee is a substance abuser, or the employee's own admission to using drugs or to drinking on the job.

Postincident and *postaccident testing* are subspecies of testing for cause. If an accident occurs on the job, test everyone involved, including all injured employees and possible violators of safety rules.

To reduce the possibility of getting sued for improper drug testing, test only for cause. Randomly testing your employees' urine when you don't have a good reason is like breaking into their homes without a search warrant. Both "searches" intrude on an individual's privacy rights. But if you suspect an employee is using drugs on the job or stealing office equipment to pay for a drug habit, the search is legal and the intrusion on privacy justified.

As I mentioned before, you're obligated to keep rotten apples out of your work force. More and more employers are using *preemployment testing* to cull out these bad apples, especially in high-risk environments.

Preemployment substance-abuse testing, like all testing, should be nondiscriminatory. Not every applicant has to take a preemployment drug test; you can save money by testing only those who advance beyond the initial interview. It's a good idea, however, to test while there are still several eligible candidates in the hiring pool. Then the test results can be a factor in the final hiring decision, but not the only factor. This type of preemployment testing diminishes the likelihood of a discrimination suit under Title VII of the Civil Rights Act of 1964.

Of Their Own Free Will

Never force an employee to take a drug test! If an employee refuses to be tested, you have the right to discipline him or her (you can link the severity of the discipline to the nature of the job or the workplace), or you can allow the employee to resign.

Many bosses think they must fire every employee who refuses to undergo testing. This makes sense if, for instance, an employee working under the influence endangers the safety of other workers or the public. But it may not be the right procedure for your company. Instead, you might prefer to implement a policy that employees cannot come to work until they have been tested. Numerous absences from work due to repeated refusals to undergo testing would then be grounds for disciplinary action.

Regardless of which line you take, be sure to explain the policy carefully to your employees.

Testing and Unions

Because drug testing is a matter of employee safety and health, it's bound to come up in collective bargaining sessions with unions. The union may demand that you bargain with its representatives before you implement a testing program. And you'll almost certainly have to bargain if you plan to discipline or fire employees for having positive test results.

Results of arbitration in labor disputes involving workplace drug use have been inconsistent. For instance, arbitrators recently overturned the firing of an employee who refused to undergo drug testing as part of an annual medical examination. So, if you want to establish a testing program in a union shop, talk to the union reps first. A little preemptive bargaining now can avoid a messy labor dispute later.

PRIVATE MATTERS

You've set up a sensible substance abuse policy. You're happy with your drug and alcohol testing program. Your employees know that using drugs or alcohol on the job can lead to disciplinary action or termination. What can possibly go wrong?

Well, an employee might sue you for invasion of privacy. Believe it or not, that's the number one hazard of work force testing programs.

An employer who doesn't know how privacy protection works, or who blatantly ignores employee privacy rights in the crusade against on-the-job substance abuse, can undo the most carefully wrought initiative. It's easy to avoid invasion-of-privacy hassles, however, if you know where your legal risks lie.

Implicit Rights

Even though the U.S. Constitution does not explicitly state that citizens have a right to privacy, the Supreme Court has recognized an implicit individual privacy guarantee in the Bill of Rights. So far, no one has tried to use this privacy guarantee to keep an employer from investigating or searching (testing) an employee suspected of using drugs or alcohol on the job.

But the Supreme Court *has* cited Constitutional privacy guarantees in other cases involving employee privacy. For instance, it has stated that employees can ask employers to maintain the confidentiality of sensitive information in personnel files. Thus, employers don't have to give the psychological test results of individual employees to unions during collective bargaining; a statistical summary of all employees' results will do. It wouldn't be going too far to extend this line of judicial reasoning to the results of individual employees' substance abuse tests.

What the States Say

Unlike the U.S. Constitution, some state constitutions guarantee the privacy rights of individuals. Since 1971, article I, section 1 of the California constitution has declared that all citizens have a right to life, liberty, safety, happiness, and *privacy*. The constitutions of Alaska, Arizona, Florida, Massachusetts, Montana, and Rhode Island contain similar privacy guarantees. If your state isn't on this list, it may be among those considering the addition of a privacy protection clause to their constitutions.

No matter where your organization is located, its substance abuse testing program shouldn't infringe on employee privacy rights. Do everything right from the start, and you'll be covered if your state eventually does decide to make privacy protection a constitutional imperative.

Common-Law Privacy

The common law protects privacy in several ways. For example, an employee can sue an employer for disclosing sensitive information such as salary figures, medical data, performance evaluations, and substance abuse test results. You can be sued if you spread this information around without having a good reason, or if you give it to people who don't need to know it. It's best to keep sensitive information confidential to prevent embarrassing intrusions on your employees' privacy that could snowball into litigation.

Your employees have private lives both on and off the job. The common law says that anything employees do on their own time is their business. But the common law doesn't take into account that many drugs can cause substantial impairment for hours or even days after ingestion, creating possible safety hazards and performance problems in the workplace.

Some employers are going against the common-law grain by testing for off-site substance abuse. Such testing is justified, they feel, because off-the-job abuse may indicate serious instability that is inconsistent with acceptable job performance.

How you deal with your employees' off-the-job substance abuse should depend on how the abuse affects their work. You might get in trouble if you discipline or fire an employee who has a couple of drinks or who smokes marijuana over the weekend, because you will probably have a hard time demonstrating any correlation between the substance abuse and the employee's job performance. The court would probably back you up, however, if you disciplined or fired an employee who made a multimillion-dollar error because he or she came to work with a raging hangover.

Who Needs to Know?

Many employers make problems for themselves by mishandling requests for information about employee substance abuse. This privacy issue really comes down to who gets the information—and why.

Department Managers. Sharing confidential employee information among departments can lead to serious problems. To keep such information from getting into the wrong hands for the wrong reasons, instruct department heads to ask a couple of simple questions:

1. Does the person requesting the information really need to know?
2. What does he or she intend to do with it?

If a manager from one department asks for the drug test results of an employee from another department, that manager had better have an ironclad reason for the request. Employee information that one department has gathered for a particular purpose should not go to another department that plans to use the information for an entirely different purpose.

Information about employees is confidential, and so is information *from* employees. If a department opts to share such material with other departments, it should delete references to the identity of employee information sources before it passes on the documents.

Unions.   Put on kid gloves when you handle union requests for information about employee substance abuse in your organization. Here are some guidelines:

1. Don't provide such information unless you and the union obtain the employee's permission to release it.
2. If you don't get permission, tell the union that you will not provide the requested records unless you can delete the employee's name and identifying characteristics from them.
3. If you cannot protect the identity of employees by deleting information in their records, offer the union a summary document, such as a statistical listing.

Defamation Dangers

Just when you think it's safe to give employee test results and substance abuse records to others, along comes a defamation suit.

Karin E.'s drug test is positive for cocaine use. You spread the word among her clients and your company's department heads that she is a "coke head." A confirmation test, however, shows that the first test was wrong. Karin sues you, claiming that you have tarnished her business and personal reputation. The moral: Make sure any information you give out concerning employee substance abuse is absolutely correct.

Defamation is called *libel* if the communication is written and *slander* if the communication is oral. No matter how the information is disseminated, truth is always the best defense against defamation charges. Because of the margin of error in substance abuse testing, be very careful not to tell others about employees' positive results unless they've been confirmed.

ABUSERS HAVE RIGHTS

Privacy isn't the only legal quagmire for employers who try to curb on-the-job substance abuse. Federal and state laws protect the rights of drug addicts and alcoholics, and if employers violate these laws, they can get into the same kind of trouble that violation of any fair-employment statute would cause.

Federal Rehabilitation Act of 1973

Among the physically and mentally challenged workers protected by this act are substance abusers. There are only two exceptions: if an employee's current use of alcohol or drugs impedes the performance of his or her job, or if the employee's substance abuse directly threatens the safety or property of others.

You cannot discipline or fire substance-abusing employees just because they are alcoholics or drug addicts. But if an employee's alcoholism or drug addiction leads to excessive absenteeism, unsatisfactory job performance, or disruptive or dangerous behavior, you have the right to treat that employee exactly as you would other workers who break the rules.

You might think there's a bit of a paradox here. The act prohibits discrimination in employment against substance abusers who are otherwise qualified for a job. Yet if you hire even a highly qualified substance abuser, aren't you setting yourself up for a negligent hiring suit down the line?

Not necessarily. The Rehabilitation Act of 1973 actually states that you cannot discriminate against *recovered* alcoholics and drug users because they have a history of substance abuse. The act protects only substance abusers who have been rehabilitated or who are undergoing rehabilitation. It does not protect unregenerate substance abusers who have not sought treatment.

The act encourages employers to help qualified employees overcome their substance-abuse problems—for instance, by giving them time off to go to treatment centers or attend substance abuse counseling programs. In general, the act states that you must do what you can to reasonably accommodate the limitations of all physically or mentally challenged employees unless the accommodation might hinder day-to-day business activity.

Section 503 of the act applies to all federal government agencies, as well as to contractors and subcontractors with federal contracts over $2,500. Only the Office of Federal Contract Compliance Programs can enforce section 503; physically and mentally challenged individuals can't bring suits on their own. But they can sue under section 504, which bars discrimination against physically or mentally challenged recipients of federal financial aid.

Title VII of the Civil Rights Act of 1964

You think you're going after substance abusers; instead, you get sued for discrimination. How does this happen?

Policies aimed at halting alcohol and drug abuse in the workplace may violate Title VII if they seem to zero in on a particular racial, religious, or ethnic group. So, even though statistics may show that certain groups protected by Title VII are more likely to use drugs, don't limit your testing only to members of those groups. If you do, you're a sitting duck for a discrimination case.

Until recently, Title VII protected religious activities involving drug use. Then, in a dramatic reversal, the Supreme Court upheld the firing of two Indian social workers for using peyote in Native American Church rituals. (This stand may have been prompted because the two were drug counselors.) But the court also left a loophole: States can still pass laws permitting employees to participate in religious drug use as long as it takes place away from the work site and does not impede productivity.

Title VII does allow you to implement substance-abuse policies that might otherwise seem discriminatory if you can prove that such policies are essential to the operation of your business.

State Laws

Most states echo the federal government in prohibiting discrimination against physically and mentally challenged employees; however, not all states consider substance abuse a handicap. Consult the laws for your state before developing substance abuse policies or testing programs.

In some states, a growing number of state workers' compensation appeal boards are awarding benefits to employees who claim that they are disabled because of drinking problems brought on by job stress. The boards are justifying their awards on the grounds that the employees have suffered an occupational injury (nervous tension), culminating in total disability.

If this trend catches on nationally, it could lead to a general recognition of alcohol and drug abuse as occupational illnesses—like asbestosis or black lung—or as by-products of occupational stress. That would mean a dramatic rise in the number of employees entitled to compensation and treatment under workers' compensation laws.

NEGLIGENCE PITFALLS

Sometimes what you don't do can cause more harm than what you actually do wrong. Smart lawyers know how to use employers' sins of omission against them in termination cases involving employee substance abuse. For example, several courts have awarded damages to employees because their former employers negligently and inaccurately maintained their medical records.

Moreover, there is an emerging but solid line of decisions in which judges have held employers responsible for *negligent supervision or retention* of incompetent or dangerous employees. Substance abusers may fall into both categories. Therefore, you should keep a close eye on possible or known abusers who might present a hazard to their co-workers. Failure to supervise problem employees carefully (especially known substance abusers) can leave you wide open to negligence litigation.

Don't let compassion or fear compel you to keep a truly dangerous individual in your work force, especially if he or she refuses to undergo treatment. Retaining such employees is usually a one-way ticket to a negligence suit.

EMPLOYERS AS COPS

Earlier, I mentioned that you have the right to search employees' property and to question them if you suspect on-site substance abuse. That doesn't mean, however, that you should behave as if you were auditioning for "Miami Vice." Brutality and coercion may earn ratings points for TV cops, but they spell trouble for real-life law enforcement officials. More to the point, they can get employers sued.

Employee Searches

As I explained in Chapter 3, searching for contraband in employee lockers, automobiles, desks, or work areas is legitimate *as long as you obtain the consent of the employees involved.* But barging into employee property without consent is an invasion of privacy. Recently, a Texas jury awarded an employee $108,000 because her employer did a random search of company lockers, including hers, during a workplace substance abuse investigation.

Arrests and Interrogations

Can you legally make a citizen's arrest and detain a substance-abusing employee until the police arrive? Yes, but only under these circumstances:

1. The employee commits a misdemeanor in your presence.
2. The employee commits a felony, in or out of your presence.
3. A felony has been committed, and you have good reason to believe that the employee committed it.

In many states drug abuse is a felony, so you can make a citizen's arrest if an employee is obviously and seriously impaired by drugs. Again, limit such arrests to situations in which safety or security demands that you detain the employee until the police arrive.

Employers who go a little crazy in making citizen's arrests might be accused of *false imprisonment,* or illegally hampering the liberty of an individual. False imprisonment occurs if you use your authority as an employer, or if you physically restrain an employee, to prevent him or her from leaving an area.

Overly zealous interrogation of suspected substance abusers often leads to a claim of false imprisonment. So, if you're investigating substance abuse at your company, allow all employees—even those with positive test results—to enter and leave company premises freely.

Try not to intimidate employees when you question them, either. Don't ever hit an employee, and don't compel him or her to confess to on-the-job substance abuse or any other crime. Assault (attempting to commit bodily harm) and battery (using force or violence) are not legitimate investigative tools. If you ignore my advice and resort to strong-arm tactics, don't be surprised if the subject of your interrogation sues you for intentional infliction of emotional distress.

YOUR DAY IN COURT

Push can come to shove when you're dealing with drinking and drug use in the workplace; there may be nothing left to do except to fire an abuser. Because we live in the Age of Litigation, the fired employee will probably take you to court. How should you prepare for a termination case involving workplace substance abuse?

Most arbitrators and courts will want to know whether an employer's grounds for firing an employee are sound. Therefore, you must present clear, hard evidence that the employee has abused drugs or alcohol in the workplace; a suspicion of on-the-job abuse is never good enough.

Employers often rely on the testimony of supervisory personnel to provide proof of employee substance abuse. Unless your supervisors are trained to detect substance abuse, however, the defense attorney will rip their testimony to shreds. Arbitrators and judges require *substantive* evidence, which usually means a positive drug or alcohol test, or testimony from someone skilled in detecting employee substance abuse.

Judges and arbitrators will also expect you to produce clear, explicit policies that explain what supervisory personnel should do if an employee appears to be using alcohol or drugs on the job. Of course, a policy can't be very effective if supervisors don't put it into practice, so you must be able to show that your supervisors have appropriate guidelines for handling employee substance abuse, and that they're actually following those guidelines.

In termination cases that challenge your testing procedures, be prepared to demonstrate the following:

1. The test had some connection with job performance.
2. The employee knew about the test ahead of time.
3. The employee knew what would happen if he or she refused to undergo testing.
4. The test results were kept confidential.
5. The testing was not discriminatory.

To gain an unbiased assessment of the evidence and make sure that you have followed in-house procedures correctly, your supervisor should review the facts of the case. A review of the evidence by your company's legal counsel can also help ensure consistency with procedures, as well as minimizing the possibility of errors.

What It Takes to Win

If you want a judge to agree that you had no alternative except to fire an employee for drinking or drug abuse, you must prove that:

1. The substance abuse had an adverse effect on your company's operations.
2. The abuse impeded other workers' efficiency.
3. The abuse hurt your relations with customers.
4. The abuse directly threatened your property or assets.

In general, the judge is likely to uphold the firing if you can show that substance abuse, whether in or out of the workplace, affected an employee's job performance or presented a threat to the safety of his or her co-workers.

There's one sure way to lose a drug- or drinking-related termination case: Apply a double standard to employee substance abuse incidents. In too many companies, substance-abusing managers receive a slap on the wrist while lower-level workers are harshly disciplined or fired. Inequitable procedures for handling employee substance abuse problems will not encourage the judge to see things your way, no matter how good a case you may have.

A CHECKLIST FOR SUCCESS

Here is a "cookbook" for a successful employee substance abuse program that should cover all the bases and keep you out of court.

Planning

Before implementing a program, develop policies that address:

1. How to educate employees about the program and the dangers of workplace substance abuse.
2. How to train supervisors to detect and deal with employee substance abuse.
3. Which substances are prohibited.
4. Which employees will be tested, and when.
5. Which initial and confirmation tests will be used.
6. How to obtain employee consent and handle refusals to undergo testing.
7. How to establish a chain of custody for test specimens.
8. What kind of rehabilitation assistance will be offered to employees with positive tests.
9. What will happen to employees who continue to abuse drugs or alcohol after treatment.

Communication

Tell your employees about the program by explaining it in:

1. Posted signs and notices.
2. Employee handbooks and personnel materials.
3. Staff memoranda.
4. Supervisor and employee training classes.
5. Written policy statements.

Consent

Keep testing voluntary by making sure that employees:

1. Understand the testing procedures and their potential effect on employment status.
2. Agree to testing as a condition of employment.
3. Sign a document releasing you from claims connected with the test or its results.
4. Realize the legal implications of the test.

Handling Abusers

In general, use your program to identify and help addicts and alcoholics, not to punish them:

1. Give employees a chance to explain positive test results.
2. Don't rush to judgment without getting a confirmation test for positive results.
3. Examine both medical and lay evidence before determining whether to discipline or fire an employee for on-the-job substance abuse.
4. Don't immediately fire employees who test positive; encourage them to participate in employee assistance or treatment programs.
5. Make sure disciplinary action, if any, is in line with company policy and procedures.
6. Explain to employees who test positive or who are known abusers that on-the-job drinking or drug use is a serious problem that threatens the safety of everyone in the workplace, that help is available, and that they'll be suspended or fired if they don't take advantage of it.
7. Inform employees who enter treatment programs that they must show improvement if they don't want to be terminated.

And always follow this guideline:

Handle on-the-job substance abusers exactly the same, whether they're vice presidents or entry-level workers.

CHAPTER 5

POLICIES THAT DO THE JOB

Managers who must shell out months of back pay or big-time damages in termination lawsuits usually lay the blame on anyone but themselves. They claim that they lost because the other side's lawyers knew how to hog-tie and hornswoggle the judge, or because the courts always side with poor, defenseless employees over mean, nasty bosses.

Are you ready for a hard truth? *It's your own fault if you get into termination trouble.* No employer wants to pay a fat settlement to a litigious employee with a smart lawyer. Without the right discipline and termination policies, you're likely to find your company pocketbook several hundred thousand dollars lighter. And far too many companies don't have the right discipline and termination policies.

Without carefully drawn internal procedures for every aspect of employment, no one really knows what's going on. Supervisors without guidelines will end up handling similar situations very differently. Employees notice that discipline is inconsistent and that firings seem to discriminate against one group or another. They become confused and angry, and they start knocking on attorneys' doors. Another hard truth: Poor communication leads to litigation.

Want to avoid such problems? Just develop clear, concise policies that cover the entire employment process, and make sure they're followed.

IT ALL BEGINS WITH HIRING

When you hire a new employee, the last thing on your mind is discipline or termination. Many employers don't realize that casual comments made during a job interview can provoke serious legal aftershocks in a termination suit. Also, a bright, shiny new worker may quickly become tarnished—and that means disciplinary action or firing. Bad hires always come back to haunt you in one way or another.

Good hiring policies can prevent later firing problems. For maximum protection, your hiring procedures should address two major issues: culling out the bad apples while avoiding any appearance of discrimination, and maintaining your firing rights by salvaging as much of the at-will relationship as the law will allow.

Screen Your Screening Policies

Some employers are the most trusting people in the world: They actually believe everything on a prospective employee's job application or résumé. Actually, few employers dig as deeply into an applicant's background as they should.

Doing a thorough background check on every new hire may seem like a waste of time and money. Look at it this way: It makes more sense to spend your resources on screening to find the best possible employees than on fighting bad ex-employees in firing disputes.

But hiring has its booby traps, too. You certainly don't need to incur a hiring-related lawsuit in the process of avoiding firing problems, so you must be aware of the legal quirks of applicant screening. Here are some good general guidelines:

1. Scan the application form carefully for red flags such as lack of professional references, fake addresses, conflicting employment dates, and peculiar reasons for leaving jobs. Also, make sure the applicant hasn't skipped any parts of the application, and that he or she has signed it.
2. Ask candidates probing interview questions about their backgrounds and goals. (A question is OK legally as long as it has something to do with the job the applicant is seeking.)
3. Check references!
4. Conduct more than one interview to confirm the initial interviewer's perceptions of the applicant's abilities, motivation, initiative, and sense of responsibility.

If you decide to delve into a job applicant's background, you must obtain his or her consent (preferably written), along with a signed liability release. You can include the authorization to seek additional information and liability release in the employment application, which the applicant should complete and sign in ink before you initiate the background check.

Hiring processes tend to drag on and on. Months may elapse between receipt of a résumé and an actual job interview. Keep in mind that an applicant is responsible only for the information given on the date of the application. To be on the safe side, you should not process job applications that are more than 90 days old without interviewing or reinterviewing the prospective employee.

How deep should you dig? It all depends. Sometimes applications and résumés tell more than their writers want you to know, so watch for red flags.

Do as extensive a check as possible. For instance, if an application or résumé contains a gap between jobs of six months or longer, there may be a perfectly acceptable explanation for the lengthy period of unemployment. On the other hand, the applicant may have spent that time in a drug rehabilitation program or in prison. Whether you hire an ex-junkie or former jailbird is up to you. But you have the right to know these things before you make employment decisions.

Suppose your background check reveals that the applicant has a criminal record. Now, it's perfectly all right to hire an ex-offender, and having a criminal record is not necessarily a roadblock to employment. Again, though, you have the right to discover this kind of information before you hire.

In general, you can learn what you need to know by having applicants sign a statement in the application about felony convictions. (Remember, arrests don't count if they don't result in convictions.) Don't hesitate to find out more, however, if you suspect that an applicant may not be telling the whole truth. You might want to think twice about hiring an ex-con who tries to cover up his or her criminal record.

When an applicant has worked at a sensitive job involving money or other valuables, make sure that you learn why he or she left that job. Workers often seek new and unrelated employment after getting caught stealing or misappropriating funds from a former employer.

Another giveaway is an applicant who seems to have too much education or work experience for a particular position. Why is a former company vice president looking for a job taking care of plants? An overqualified applicant may be making a legitimate career switch—or he or she may have an employment-related skeleton in the closet. It's worth checking into.

We've all known résumé writers who deserved a Nobel prize in fiction for their work. That's why you must read between the laser-printed lines of every résumé you receive.

Some applicants give very sketchy information about former employers because those employers don't exist. Watch out for company addresses that consist of post office box numbers; if the applicant can't also supply an actual street address, the company may well be a phantom.

Another common résumé ploy is trying to get more money out of employers by inflating salary figures from previous jobs. Applicants lump in mileage allowances, bonuses, even projected pay raises. Only the base salary counts. Try to extract it from the employee, if possible; otherwise, you'll have to contact the personnel department at the employee's former company.

Hang On to Your At-Will Rights

Although the law does limit many of your rights to hire and fire at-will, you shouldn't throw away the ones you have left!

You'll avoid untold grief if you make it clear to all new employees from the start that they are employed at-will—that there's no contract, written or otherwise, stating how long they'll work for you, how much they'll make, and so on.

When recruiting or interviewing applicants, don't say anything about job security or permanent or continued employment. The minute you remark, "As long as you do your job well, you've got a job with us," you've created a contract and demolished your at-will rights. You should also remove references to "tenure," "right to continue," "termination only for just cause," "permanent employees," and the like from your recruiting brochures and personnel materials.

You may want to consider including an employment at-will statement and contract disclaimer in your company's job application forms. Such statements make it crystal-clear that:

1. Either party can sever the employment relationship, with or without a legal reason ("cause").
2. To change the at-will relationship, the employee and an authorized person from the organization must jointly sign a legal document describing the changes.
3. Oral statements by company officials do not modify the at-will relationship. Neither do personnel manuals, procedures, pension plans, and other company materials.
4. Duration of employment, favorable performance evaluations, changes in pay or other compensation, job location, and level of employment do not modify the at-will relationship.
5. The at-will relationship does not change if the employee relocates or gives something up to accept a job with the company.
6. If problems arise regarding the at-will relationship, the employer chooses the jurisdiction and forum (court, arbitration hearing) for settling disputes.

Never send a prospective employee a job offer letter that confirms employment and states annual compensation. The employee could use the letter to prove that he or she never had an at-will relationship with your company. If your letter says that you are going to pay the employee, say, $50,000 a year, the employee might get the idea that he or she is being hired for at least a year. All of a sudden, you have a year-long contract on your hands!

Whenever you talk about pay with applicants and employees, give a weekly or monthly rather than an annual figure. That way, you're explicitly referring to the rate of compensation, not implicitly specifying a period of employment.

Of course, some employers and employees do have contracts. As you might expect, contract employment is an entirely different ball game from at-will employment. I'll cover the legalities of disciplining and firing contract workers later in this book.

POLICIES WITH A POINT

You've developed and implemented hiring procedures everyone can live with. You're screening applicants carefully so that you won't have to fire almost as soon as you've hired. Now it's time to give some thought to the big guns: your disciplinary, termination, and information procedures and policies. Here are some general guidelines:

1. Make sure that your policies clearly state what will happen if employees do something wrong or perform poorly. Be particularly explicit about situations that warrant disciplinary action or termination.
2. Specify employee rights and employer responsibilities.
3. Ensure that policies are appropriate to the context of your business.
4. Develop policies that promote uniformity in managerial decision making.
5. Develop policies that help maintain good employee morale by being fair and encouraging confidence in management.
6. Develop policies that reduce the possibility of discrimination hassles and other employment disputes.
7. Publish your policies and give copies to your employees. Notify employees in a timely fashion if there are changes or updates to the policies.

Many employers are leery of putting discipline and termination policies in writing. Believe me, this approach is no trouble saver; in fact, it tends to lead to dangerous misunderstandings between supervisors and employees. If you peruse recent court cases, you will see that ignorance, misinformation, and suspicion—the by-products of not having clearly articulated procedures—are at the root of a lot of termination lawsuits.

It's sad to think of all those companies giving away their money to ex-employees and their lawyers when problems stemming from fuzzy discipline and termination policies are so easily prevented. Basically, an organization just has to develop sensible policies, state them clearly, and spread them around to the supervisors and employees they affect.

Get off to a good start by making sure that supervisory personnel receive a thorough briefing on your organization's discipline and termination procedures. Ask yourself how well your supervisors really know and understand the procedures; schedule seminars and refreshers as necessary.

All the briefings in the world don't mean a thing if your supervisors don't actually *follow* the procedures they're briefed on. You must realistically consider the possibility that supervisors won't always stick to organizational policy when they decide to discipline or terminate employees. To gauge supervisors' adherence to the company "firing line," you might have to periodically oversee and review the actions they take when they discipline or fire.

Likewise, policies and procedures aren't effective if they don't get to the right people—or if they fall into the hands of the wrong ones. Who are the right people? That depends. Do you want solely to educate and guide supervisory employees? Then distribute your discipline and termination policies only to supervisory employees. Distributing policies intended for managerial use to nonmanagerial employees may increase the risk of litigation in case a supervisor doesn't follow those policies to the letter. If, however, you want both to instruct managers and inform nonmanagerial employees, by all means distribute the policies to everyone. It might be appropriate, considering the double-headed goal here, to draft two different versions of the policies, one for supervisors and one for employees.

You may also have to test the policies and procedures to determine whether they fit the kinds of situations that are bound to arise in your organization. Many personnel policies cover the right theoretical bases, but have no application to everyday workplace realities.

BE UP FRONT WITH EMPLOYEES

Never leave your employees in the dark about what your organization considers improper behavior or grounds for dismissal. Tell employees that you have the right to discipline or fire them for specific, clearly stated reasons, such as those given in Chapter 3.

Reasons to discipline or terminate employees vary from organization to organization, but they may include:

1. Being excessively absent or chronically late to work.
2. Violating safety, security, or health rules; endangering the health or safety of co-workers and others.
3. Being negligent.
4. Being discourteous to customers.
5. Fighting with co-workers or creating a serious disturbance on company premises.
6. Being insubordinate to supervisors; refusing to do work assigned by a supervisor or delaying work output and encouraging other employees to act similarly.
7. Stealing money, property, or valuables belonging to the employer, co-workers, or members of the public.
8. Using illegal drugs or being drunk during work hours.
9. Possessing firearms or other weapons on company premises or while engaged in company business.
10. Gambling on company premises or during scheduled work time.
11. Sexually harassing employees, co-workers, or members of the public.
12. Discriminating against employees, co-workers, or members of the public because of race, religion, and so on.
13. Disclosing confidential records and other data belonging to the employer, co-workers, or customers; disclosing trade secrets to unauthorized persons.
14. Using company equipment (computers, copiers, and so on) without authorization.
15. Falsifying company documents, time sheets, personnel files, and other records.
16. Violating government regulations applicable to the job.
17. Violating the employer's code of ethics or business practices.
18. Destroying, damaging, or defacing company property (equipment, tools, products, records, information, and so on).

19. Being convicted of a crime that is directly related to or that can adversely affect ability to perform a job.

Obviously, these reasons don't carry equal weight. Some employee offenses are more serious than others, and merit heavier punishment. The chronic latecomer is hardly in the same league as the chronic cocaine sniffer; the worker who uses the company computer for personal projects is not as dangerous as the worker who sells next year's marketing plans to the competition.

So, your organization needs a sliding scale for employee offenses. It's important to distinguish between serious infractions that cry out for immediate termination and minor problems that can be handled with progressive disciplinary measures.

Never fire an employee for an employment "misdemeanor." And give supervisors some latitude to figure out whether an employee offense is truly serious.

No matter how exhaustive a list of reasons for discipline and termination you come up with, employees are bound to come up with more. Therefore, you should let employees know that your idea of unacceptable workplace behavior isn't limited to what's on the list. You have the right to expand the definition of misconduct as you see fit, and to add offenses to the list.

If your termination policies are ever put to the test in court, their validity may hinge on whether you gave employees *proper notice* of what to expect for violating your rules. Lack of notice probably causes more employers to wipe out in termination cases than anything else.

An employee suing you for wrongful discharge or something similar will probably claim that he or she didn't receive proper notice about your rules and the penalties for breaking them. You should be able to parry this defense by showing that you gave employees plenty of notice through employee handbooks, announcements on bulletin boards, memos, newsletter articles, and the like.

What if you have nothing in writing? All is not lost, as long as supervisors give employees verbal notice about offenses and sanctions.

Employee Handbook Hazards

Employee handbooks are a great way to disseminate a lot of personnel information in a convenient package. But if that information isn't phrased correctly and unambiguously, employees can misinterpret it. More than one litigious ex-employee has found rich pickings in an employee handbook.

To prevent potential legal hassles, go over your employee handbook with a fine-tooth comb and excise all references to:

1. Job security.
2. Tenure.
3. Permanent employee(s).
4. Promises to fire only for just cause.
5. Litigation involving the employer's discretion to fire.
6. Promises to follow a particular discharge procedure.
7. Promises to attempt to rehabilitate unsatisfactory employees.

Why keep these references out of the handbook? Unless you stipulate otherwise, an employee handbook is a binding document—a contract. Your at-will rights evaporate the minute a contract appears. So, if your handbook states that you will fire only for just cause, you cannot fire for any other reason. Your firing rights are restricted enough as it is. Don't toss away the ones you have left!

If you alter your handbook to eliminate references to job security or just-cause termination, you might want to sugar the pill by giving employees a wage increase or a desirable employee benefit. That way, you show that you did not delete the references to punish your employees.

A good way to circumvent such problems is to insert a prominent statement in the handbook declaring that the procedures and policies it describes are *not* contractual, and that you have the right to hire and fire at-will (within the bounds of the law, of course). You might also ask each employee to sign a separate at-will statement on receiving his or her copy of the employee handbook, and then place the signed form in the employee's personnel folder as part of his or her permanent record.

The employee handbook should clearly state that you reserve the right to amend your layoff, discipline, and termination policies to be in line with your organization's changing business needs. Whenever you revise the handbook for any reason, have each employee sign a document acknowledging receipt of the new handbook and stating that it supersedes previous versions.

Some companies, averring that employee handbooks cause more problems than they solve, have stopped using them. Instead, they've substituted supervisory manuals that describe corporate policies and procedures. Supervisory manuals have the goal of facilitating consistent treatment of employees. Whether you use a supervisory manual to accompany or replace the employee handbook, insert a disclaimer on its first page stating that your organization's policies and procedures do not represent binding contractual obligations.

Performance Review Pitfalls

If you're not reviewing the performance of your employees on a regular basis, you should be. There's no better way to tell it like it is to an employee than via a performance review. Performance evaluations give you the opportunity to catch minor problems before they become major ones; to provide employees with kudos or constructive criticism, as warranted; to ensure fairness and consistency in the way employees are treated; and to help supervisors assess candidates for advancement as well as for possible dismissal.

A performance review system is also the best way to forge an equitable relationship between raises and the kind of work employees do. It may seem like common sense to link pay and performance, but some bosses give merit increases to workers whose performance is rated as unacceptable. Then, when such workers are fired (as they almost inevitably are), they go to the judge and say, "Well, I can't be as bad as the company says I am. Look at the fat raise I got!"

Because performance reviews often determine whether an employee goes or stays, they clearly play a starring role in termination lawsuits. To keep your performance review system from tripping you up in court, follow these guidelines:

1. Make sure that supervisors understand the company's goals and the kind of performance it expects of its employees.
2. Constantly emphasize proper documentation of employee performance.
3. Remember that an employee's failure to meet goals and expectations can, when properly documented, provide a strong justification for corrective discipline.
4. Establish ties between performance reviews and progressive disciplinary action (see "Early Warning System" later in this chapter), and set an acceptable timetable for employees to correct problems pointed out in reviews.
5. Ensure that the review form contains enough categories to evaluate all applicable elements of performance.

TERMINATE WITHOUT PREJUDICE

Your termination policies should always have two goals. One is to be fair; the other, to stave off lawsuits from angry ex-employees. If you take care of the first goal, you should have no problem with the second.

Playing fair means avoiding the nefarious double standard—separate but unequal treatment of exempt and nonexempt employees—that kills so many employers in court. Internal procedures should ensure consistent treatment of employees under similar circumstances. Thus, a corporate vice president who uses illegal drugs on the job should receive exactly the same punishment as a custodian who uses illegal drugs on the job.

Fairness also hinges on facts, and it's up to you to get them. You must investigate every firing to determine that the employee is being let go because of a serious violation of your rules, not because of a supervisory whim.

How do you gauge whether a firing is fair? Having an advance review mechanism in place can help greatly. You might consider designating someone at each work site to be in charge of independently reviewing all proposed dismissals. A reviewer won't be very effective if he or she isn't well versed in your organization's personnel policies and practices, so it makes sense to appoint a personnel professional to handle this task. Naturally the reviewer should have the authority to reject a proposed termination.

Even if things reach flash point, never fire an employee on the spot. Stay cool, and remember that you can never have too many facts about a proposed termination. To bolster the personnel professional's independent review, let a higher-level manager (at least one rung higher than the employee's direct supervisor) evaluate the proposed firing.

When health or safety dictates that an employee be removed immediately from the workplace, suspend him or her and then conduct a thorough investigation. If the review leads inexorably to the conclusion that the employee must be fired, you can easily convert the suspension into a dismissal. Likewise, if firing isn't called for, you can just as easily reinstate the employee.

As always, it's best to think before you fire. Here are some good things to think about when investigating a proposed termination:

- Give the employee a chance to tell his or her side of the story (verbally or in a written statement) before you make your decision.
- Consider the employee's tenure and work record, as well as whether he or she has committed similar offenses while employed by your organization.
- Make sure that the employee doesn't have an Equal Employment Opportunity Commission discrimination suit or a workers' compensation claim pending against your company.
- Ascertain whether supervisors involved in the firing decision have followed all relevant personnel policies.

Early Warning System

When you discipline employees, the punishment must fit the crime. You can't fire every worker who breaks your rules, but you can't overlook problems, either. You need the sliding scale I mentioned earlier—a progressive disciplinary system in which you mete out increasingly severe penalties for increasingly serious or repeat offenses. Such a program can help you deal with troublesome workers before they become real thorns in your side. It can also provide a superb counterpoint to charges of bias, coercion, and discriminatory conduct in wrongful discharge suits.

I recommend a multistage approach with the following elements:

Verbal Warnings. In this mild form of discipline, the supervisor goes over the infraction with the employee, explaining exactly what the employee did wrong and what he or she must do to correct the problem. Your policies might state that an employee will receive a certain number of verbal warnings before a written warning is issued or more serious steps are taken.

Written Warnings. Written warnings can accompany or follow verbal warnings. A written warning should describe the employee's performance deficits; refer to dates when the employee received counseling; outline performance or conduct expectations and give a time frame for achieving them; and describe what will happen if the employee does not consistently meet those expectations.

The supervisor usually gives the written warning to the employee to read during a meeting or counseling session. The employee and supervisor discuss the warning, and the employee signs the document to acknowledge that he or she has received it.

Counseling. The counseling that a problem employee receives should zero in on how the problem affects job performance or conduct. The supervisor who counsels a problem employee should focus on the employee's behavior, not on the individual. Also, the supervisor should get input from the employee on how to handle the problem and how long it might take to resolve.

Probation. When a problem employee doesn't live up to the conditions set in a written warning or counseling session, it's appropriate to put him or her on probation.

A recommendation for probation includes a concise narrative of the problem employee's ongoing failure to meet performance or conduct expectations, the time frame for improvement to at least a satisfactory level, and the possibility of termination if the employee doesn't pull up his or her socks. If the employee doesn't make enough progress to warrant an extension of the probationary period, the supervisor may opt to fire him or her when the probation runs out.

Suspension.   Sometimes a supervisor has to do something short of actually firing a problem employee; sometimes a supervisor just doesn't have enough information about an employee's alleged infractions to justify a termination. In such situations, the supervisor may suspend the employee until the organization decides what to do about him or her. If an investigation determines that the employee is not guilty, he or she should be reinstated and given back pay.

Dismissal.   When an errant employee continues to perform poorly or to act up after receiving verbal and written warnings, getting counseling, and being suspended, there's no choice except to terminate him or her. Keep in mind, though, that firing is the last link in this disciplinary chain; supervisors shouldn't resort to it unless they've tried everything else and come up empty.

One thing that's vital to the success of a progressive disciplinary system is impeccable recordkeeping. For every firing, you should be able to show what went wrong at every step and why milder measures failed.

Your records should prove that:

1. The employee understood what was expected of him or her at work.
2. The employee was notified in advance of all disciplinary actions, meetings, and consequences.
3. The employee had ample opportunity to improve after being warned or put on probation.
4. Other employees received similar treatment in similar circumstances.

5. Supervisors and others consistently followed company procedures, especially discipline policy.
6. The level of discipline was appropriate.

It's Not Over 'til It's Over

Employers tend to believe that termination policy ends with the decision to let someone go. But there's more to the act of firing than telling an employee to clean out his or her desk and hit the road.

These often-overlooked loose ends include the following:

Severance Pay and Waivers.   You might want to think about offering severance pay, even if an employee isn't entitled to it, in exchange for a written release of claims involving the employee's job or termination. The courts usually approve such settlement agreements, as long as the employee knowingly and voluntarily waives his or her rights.

To make sure the employee knows what he or she is getting into, put the waiver agreement in clear, understandable language and give the employee a reasonable amount of time to consider it. Don't let an employee sign a settlement agreement unless he or she has taken it home and mulled it over for at least one night. Also, encourage the employee to consult with an attorney.

Exit Interviews.   When you fire an employee, do it politely and calmly in the context of an exit interview. Always have more than one manager present so that he or she can corroborate what happened during the interview. And be sure to tell the employee exactly why he or she is being fired; don't hem and haw. (If you've followed my recommendations for a progressive discipline scheme, the firing should come as no great surprise to the employee.)

Recommendations.   Lawyers who counsel terminated employees usually suggest that the employee obtain a "letter of recommendation" from his or her former employer. People are afraid or unwilling to give bad recommendations, even to bad employees. That works to the ex-employee's favor, of course, because the lawyer can use a favorable or neutral letter of recommendation to discredit the employer's explanation for dismissing the employee.

To protect your organization from the recommendation trap, tell supervisors not to issue letters of recommendation or sign statements that glowingly describe a former employee without first checking with the personnel department.

Restrictive Covenants. Trade secrets are swapped like Wall Street commodities these days, and disgruntled former employees are often the most avid brokers of sensitive information. A restrictive covenant is a legal mechanism for ensuring that an ex-employee won't divulge confidential information about your company's products and plans to a new employer or the competition.

Some states seem to look more kindly on restrictive covenants than others. But almost all states agree that such an agreement should not be overly broad (for instance, keeping a former programmer from working for any company that uses mainframe computers), and that it shouldn't try to cover too great a geographic expanse or time period (keeping an employee from working for any company in the United States for 10 years). And, as always, a restrictive covenant should not appear discriminatory, offend public policy, or bump up against local laws.

Separation Agreements. You're probably thinking, "Arrgghh! Another piece of paper?" Yes, but a most important one. Because it covers many things that employers and employees frequently take for granted, it can do a superb job of staving off litigation. The employee can't very well argue with what's in black and white.

To cover all the bases, a separation agreement should give the following information:

1. Last day of employment.
2. Unused vacation pay.
3. Eligibility for bonuses, commissions, and other compensation.

4. Distribution of proceeds for savings or pension plans.
5. Conversion of life or medical insurance coverage, if applicable.
6. Repayment of outstanding loans, if applicable.
7. Repayment arrangement for outstanding advances (salary, travel expenses).
8. Tax consequences of the settlement.
9. Reemployment rights.

MAKING THE COURTS HAPPY

Even the best termination policies can come under legal attack. Wearing a bulletproof vest doesn't stop people from shooting at you.

Whenever you fire an employee, you've got to be prepared for the possibility of being sued. The best defense is knowing what makes the courts side with employees in termination suits.

The longer an employee has worked for an organization, the more suspect a sudden disciplinary action or termination will appear—and the more sympathetic a judge, jury, or arbitrator will be to the employee. It's even fishier when an employer fires a long-time employee who has a record of satisfactory or good performance studded with regular merit raises and promotions.

Poor or no documentation for a termination is often a red flag to the courts, especially if an employer regularly does written performance reviews. That's why I keep telling you to document all the events leading up to every termination.

Employers who don't follow their own personnel policies give terminated employees a golden opportunity to claim breach of contract and lack of good faith. Not hewing to policy also undercuts the employer's justification for firing the employee.

You won't get any Brownie points from a judge or arbitrator if you fire an employee shortly after he or she refuses to do something that violates public policy. The same goes for firing a whistle-blower or an employee who files charges or testifies against your organization. Under these circumstances, termination looks an awful lot like retaliation.

The best way to make the courts happy is to treat employees fairly and consistently in similar situations. The best way to do that is by developing sensible discipline and termination policies and making sure they're followed.

Termination policies should be clear and equitable. And they should protect the rights of everyone concerned— including the employer.

CHAPTER 6

LAWYERS, EMPLOYEES, AND MONEY

Not every employee you fire is going to sue you. But I can guarantee that the ones who do will be out for blood and money—*your* blood and money.

As I said in the last chapter, there may be chinks in even the best discipline and termination policies. So, it's not outside the realm of possibility that action by a terminated employee will put you in the thick of a lawsuit, an arbitration procedure, or a government agency investigation.

Employers have widely varying reactions to termination lawsuits. Some are cynical: "The courts always side with employees in these things, so why bother putting up a fight?" Some are nonchalant: "What, me worry? Let the lawyers handle it. After all, that's what we pay them to do." Some are belligerent: "How dare that so-and-so try to sue me? I'll nail him to the wall!" And some are reasonable: "Let's sit down and examine our defenses and options before we do anything."

Unfortunately, most employers enter the fray without a clue about what their best defenses and options might be. Many are legal greenhorns who've never even been in traffic court, let alone embroiled in an employer-employee dispute. That's why I'm going to tell you what to expect if you get socked with a discriminatory termination or wrongful discharge suit, how to handle roundhouse punches from the employee's attorneys, and, most important, how to keep from getting knocked out in the courtroom or arbitration chamber.

WHERE'S THE DISCRIMINATION?

Computer professionals Marliss G., Kurt L., and Fred P. were fired from their jobs at Foobaron International. They lodged a discrimination complaint against the company, alleging that Foobaron got rid of them because they were white Americans in their 40s. Foobaron had replaced them with three young Asian computer science hotshots.

Marliss, Kurt, and Fred asked for $70 million in compensatory and punitive damages. Their brief claimed that they were the victims of "pernicious and malicious race, age, and national origin discrimination." Strong language . . . but true? Not necessarily.

The vast majority of employees who file a discrimination suit do *not* have a legitimate claim! When an employer disciplines or fires an employee, the employee almost always thinks that the employer has treated him or her unfairly—that's just human nature. Now, if the person who is disciplined or fired happens to be a woman, a member of a minority group, or over the age of 40, the employer's actions may start smelling like discrimination, especially to a canny lawyer. Rest assured, however, that no court or arbitrator is going to rule in favor of an employee who tries to pull an unjustified discrimination number to get back at an employer for firing him or her.

Even though there are a lot of antidiscrimination laws that employees attempt to use against employers, there are also laws that give employers an edge in the courtroom. In many jurisdictions, for instance, you still have the right to discipline or fire employees for almost any reason (or for no reason) as long as your motives aren't discriminatory. Unless you goof badly, you should have little trouble proving that you didn't intend to discriminate when you disciplined or fired a member of a group protected by law.

So, if Foobaron can prove that it let Marliss, Kurt, and Fred go because their work was excruciatingly awful, not because it wanted to replace them with Asians, the judge will probably let the terminations stand. Remember, proof can make or break a case.

Because discrimination cases are often tried in the federal

arena, attorneys for ex-employees tend not to rush to sue former employers. The reason is that Rule 11 of the Federal Rules of Civil Procedures stipulates that:

1. An employee's lawyer must thoroughly investigate the facts of a discrimination complaint before filing a federal suit.
2. The lawyer must make a reasonable inquiry into the applicable law.
3. The lawyer cannot sign any document intended to belabor proceedings, harass the employer, or increase the cost of litigation.

Accountability also makes employees' attorneys think twice about suing employers: Attorney and employee may both be in serious trouble if their discriminatory termination claim turns out to be groundless. Because charges of racism carry such a tremendous stigma, say the courts, such charges should be leveled only after careful investigation and thoughtful deliberation—never without a reasonable basis in both law and fact.

A smart lawyer is going to put all potential discrimination claims under the legal microscope. A less smart lawyer, perhaps a naive, idealistic sort who sees every employer as Snidely Whiplash and every employee as Little Nell, may simply believe the employee's tales of the employer's misdeeds. Unfortunately, taking a client's word at face value isn't good enough anymore. To satisfy the courts, attorneys must question their clients thoroughly. An attorney can no longer accept his or her client's version as gospel, especially if an investigation indicates that the client might be hedging on the truth.

When the EEOC Steps In

Let's say that Marliss, Kurt, and Fred have engaged a smart lawyer, Bella C. She thinks there's something to their discriminatory firing claim, so she decides to get the Equal Employment Opportunity Commission (EEOC) in on the act.

After Bella files discrimination charges against Foobaron with the EEOC, the agency processes the claim. Then it embarks on its own investigation. Just as an attorney can't take an employee's word that an employer has discriminated, the EEOC can't take an attorney's word that a case has merit.

To check out the facts of the claim, the EEOC subpoenas supervisors, personnel staff, and other Foobaron employees who might know about the firing of Marliss, Kurt, and Fred. When the EEOC subpoenas someone, it follows standards established by the National Labor Relations Act, judicial rulings, and the EEOC's own decisions.

The EEOC can uncover a lot in its investigations—more than most attorneys can dig up on their own. In fact, the commission is often a fertile source of information for employees' attorneys.

Before the EEOC can share anything with Bella, however, she must give the agency a *representation letter*. Once the EEOC has this letter, it will cooperate with Bella by providing her with most of the information it unearths.

Bella, as we said, is a smart lawyer, so she opts to let the EEOC do most of the legwork at this stage. That's because the EEOC, unlike Bella, can take statements from individuals protected under the "informant's privilege," at least for as long as the EEOC is investigating the case.

The EEOC investigation gives Bella and her three clients unparalleled powers of discovery: They can learn as much as they need to without having to file a lawsuit. This is a practical and inexpensive way for employees' attorneys to assess their cases. After the EEOC does its digging, Bella may agree that Marliss, Kurt, and Fred were hapless victims of age and ethnic discrimination—or she may decide that Foobaron had every reason in the world to fire them.

You can see how smart lawyers use the EEOC to employees' advantage. The EEOC will give the claimant's attorney all kinds of information that would otherwise be difficult to come by. The employer's counsel, on the other hand, won't even be able to learn who gave statements to the EEOC during its investigation.

Attorneys Play Hardball

Of course, Bella isn't going to sit around and wait for the EEOC's report to float across her desk; she's also going to conduct her own investigation. It's very unusual for an employee's attorney to put off fact gathering until after the EEOC has filed a discrimination complaint.

The first thing Bella will do is analyze Foobaron International's employment practices. She'll review the company's employment manuals and policy guidelines, as well as the personnel files for Marliss, Kurt, and Fred. In the process of gathering facts for the case, she may discover other employment-related problems, such as defamation claims, violations of the Wage and Hour Act, and widespread patterns of discrimination.

After she's gone over the paperwork, Bella may decide to contact witnesses. (Again, she's not likely to sit on her hands until the EEOC files charges.) She knows that employees seldom win discrimination cases on circumstantial evidence alone. A successful settlement is usually the result of a "smoking gun," a third party who can testify that he or she heard the employer make disparaging remarks or do something discriminatory.

Will Bella identify and contact such individuals before Foobaron even finds out that they're involved in the case? Does it rain in the rain forest?

If Foobaron doesn't want to lose, it'll do a little digging of its own and find out who the "smoking guns" are before Bella does. Too many employers blow discrimination cases because they let employees' attorneys grab all the good witnesses!

Time Is on Your Side

Are you automatically in the Dumpster if an employee files a discrimination complaint against you with the EEOC? Probably not. EEOC filing is a slow, tortuous process, and its intricacies can actually work in your favor.

Keep in mind that the Age Discrimination in Employment Act (ADEA) and Title VII of the Civil Rights Act of 1964 require employees to file charges with the EEOC within 180 days of the alleged discrimination. In states that have "deferral agencies" (homegrown, state-level versions of the EEOC), employees must file charges with the EEOC no later than 300 days after the illegal practice occurred or within 30 days after the state ends its proceedings, whichever comes first.

Under the ADEA, the earliest that an employee can file a lawsuit is 60 days after filing a discrimination claim with the EEOC. The latest is two years after the alleged violation has occurred. If an employee files suit because of an employer's "willful violation" of the act, however, the employee has up to three years to sue the employer. You can use this valuable time to find and interview your own witnesses, prepare your documentation, and punch holes in the employee's case.

In a Title VII case, the EEOC usually issues a "right-to-sue" letter before the employee can file a suit. The employee may demand a formal right-to-sue letter from the EEOC 180 days after the date that charges were filed. As long as an employee is entitled to receive a right-to-sue letter, the employee doesn't have to have physical possession of the letter to get the suit rolling. But he or she must file suit within 90 days after receiving the letter.

YOUR COURT STRATEGY

When an employee sues you for discriminatory discipline or firing, you must try to think like a judge. That doesn't mean you should rush out to enroll in night school law courses. It does mean you have to pick the case apart and examine it for logical lapses, missing ingredients, and other sources of legal quicksand (see Table 6–1). You must also have some idea of what the employee is going to be hitting you with; it shouldn't come as an unpleasant surprise.

A discrimination-based termination or discipline suit always begins with the employee's complaint. Complaints are designed to make you look as bad as possible as quickly as possible; after all, the complaint is the first thing the judge reads. Unless the employee's lawyer is a tyro who has never handled a discrimination case before, the complaint will contain the following elements:

1. A statement giving the nature of the complaint.
2. A statement concerning the basis for the court's jurisdiction in the matter. (Is the court an appropriate forum? Does state or federal law apply?)

TABLE 6–1

Factors Influencing the Outcome of Employee Lawsuits

Factor	Comment
Plaintiff	Appearance, demeanor, socioeconomic background
Defendant	Individual or corporation, standing in community, reputation
Witnesses	Appearance, demeanor, socioeconomic background
"Red flags"	Length of fired employees's service with organization
	Long service combined with documented record of good performance, raises, promotions
	Absence of documentation for firing, especially if employer does regular, written performance reviews
	Sudden or unexplained decay in employee's performance just before termination, suggesting fabricated or unjustified basis for termination
	Failure of employer to follow written or customary discipline and termination policies.
	Disparate or inconsistent treatment of employees in similar situations
	Employer's use of inflammatory language or inappropriate behavior in firing the employee; derogatory references to employee's age, race, or sex
Procedural issues	Plaintiff's compliance with all requirements for bringing suit
	Extent of damage to the plaintiff
	Likelihood of favorable verdict; potential verdict range
Cost	Need for and cost of expert witnesses
	Cost of preparing and trying case

3. A statement identifying the parties involved, as well as a brief description of the reasons for invoking the law. For example, the employee must allege that he or she belongs to a group protected by Title VII or the ADEA, and that your organization is engaged in an "industry affecting commerce" and has at least 20 employees.

4. A statement that the employee has done everything required by law before going to court, such as filing discriminination charges with the EEOC or with a state deferral agency, if applicable.

5. A statement that the EEOC has investigated the case and determined that discrimination has occurred—or that it hasn't.

6. An allegation in an ADEA case that 60 days have elapsed since the filing of charges, or, in a Title VII case, that 180 days have elapsed since the filing of charges.
7. An allegation that the employee has obtained a right-to-sue letter and has gone to court within 90 days of receiving the letter.
8. A general narrative of the facts leading to the suit. If there are particularly egregious facts, the complaint must recite them and provide supporting documentation, usually as an attachment.
9. A statement that the employer has continued to discriminate since the date of the original discriminatory act, and that the employer has not complied with the requirements of Title VII or the ADEA.
10. Where appropriate, a statement that the employer's acts were "willful, knowing, intentional, and deliberate." (This allegation is a must in ADEA cases.)

If any of these elements is missing from the complaint, your attorneys may be able to do in the employee's case during their initial challenges.

The complaint will also contain a "prayer for relief," which is *not* a lawyer's plea to the Supreme Being for help with his or her case! The "prayer" will probably ask the judge to rule that you violated the ADEA or Title VII so that the employee can receive restitution ("relief") to the extent allowed by either law.

Don't be fazed by the amount and type of relief the employee's lawyer asks you to provide. As in any case involving money and damages, the other side will try to get as much out of you as they can—but that doesn't necessarily mean they'll receive everything they ask for.

Here are some examples of relief that lawyers have requested in discrimination cases:

1. Restoration of health and accident insurance, as well as reimbursement for all premiums or claims the employee had to pay because he or she didn't have the insurance.
2. Payment of the value of a company car or other benefits lost as a result of the discriminatory discipline or termination.

3. Payment of lost overtime.
4. Payment of sales commissions.
5. Payment of "front pay." When an employee is unjustly fired or denied a promotion because of discrimination, the court may order the employer to reinstate or promote him or her; however, there may be no slots for the employee to fill. Front pay, then, is the salary for the job the employee expects to fill when something appropriate opens up. It's anticipated lost wages.
6. Damages equal to (and in addition to) the amount of back pay awarded.

The prayer for relief may request that the employee be reinstated at work with full seniority, pensions, and fringe benefits, just as if he or she had never left. And the employee may seek lost wages—including raises—from the date of the discriminatory discipline or firing to the date of reinstatement.

The employee's lawyer may also try to get an injunction to prohibit your organization from violating the antidiscrimination laws in the future, and to compel you to restore the employee to his or her rightful place in the organization and the work force.

Voyage of Discovery

If you read true-crime books or watch TV cop shows, you've doubtless come across the term *rights of discovery*. Usually it refers to the rights of the defendant in a criminal trial to examine the prosecution's evidence. Basically, this privilege gives the defense a bird's-eye view of the case the plaintiff is going to present. Even though the prosecution has the tougher job— proving that the defendant committed the crime of which he or she is accused—the prosecutor does not enjoy the defense's discovery privileges. As a result, the prosecuting attorney usually has to second-guess the defense's game plan.

Now, in a wrongful discharge case involving a discrimination claim, the employee is the plaintiff (the person bringing the suit) and you're the defendant. You'd think, judging from what I just said, that you'd have the same rights of discovery as a defendant in a criminal case. Not so, unfortunately. What many employers don't realize is that in discrimination cases, the courts tend to give the employee/plaintiff broader discovery rights than usual because it's so difficult to obtain direct evidence of discrimination. And you'd better believe that plaintiffs in wrongful discharge cases exercise their discovery rights as if they were training for a marathon.

The employee's attorney will probably try to get hold of data that you might consider "classified," such as the makeup of your work force and information about your general employment practices. In recent cases, the courts have compelled employers to produce the names and locations of facilities other than the one directly associated with the suit; data on other employment discrimination complaints; termination statistics; employment qualification tests; employment applications; and information on suits and investigations involving the employer. Nothing is sacred.

Most judges won't demand that you turn over your affirmative action plans to an employee's attorney. Still, some judicial decisions have forced employers to provide the statistical background for their plans.

Employees' attorneys are pretty clever about bundling into their complaints such annoyances as "interrogatories," or formal questions. As discovery tools, interrogatories are formidable: A properly framed interrogatory question will ask you to give the factual basis for every defense you plan to use, to give supporting documentation for each defense, and to identify individuals who know anything about each defense.

The employee's attorney may also file a deposition notice with the complaint. That means you must provide testimony about the matters outlined in the notice before the case even goes to trial; this testimony may not take place in a courtroom, but it's almost always written down. When a corporate defendant receives a deposition notice, the company must designate an officer or spokesperson to testify on its behalf.

The purpose of all this, of course, is for the employee/plaintiff to find out as much as possible before you can start exercising your own discovery rights. Keep in mind, however, that both the plaintiff and the defendant must have a *legal and factual basis* for everything they do. The employee is sunk if he or she tries to pry information out of you that has no bearing on the case, just as you're sunk if you try to mount a defense that has no grounding in law or reality.

EXPERTS AND NUMBERS

In many wrongful discharge cases involving discrimination charges, plaintiffs rely heavily on expert witnesses and statistical data. Experts' testimony may change depending on who is paying them, and statistics are often as malleable as Silly Putty. But that doesn't mean they won't convince a judge or jury. So, you must be prepared to counter the employee/plaintiff's case with your own experts and statistical evidence.

What kinds of experts might you have to deal with? If the case involves an analysis of tests your company uses or a statistical evaluation of adverse-impact data, count on seeing a bevy of industrial psychologists in court. Likewise, if damages are an issue, someone will probably call in an expert to calculate anticipated damages in terms of their present value, or to quantify lost pension or social security benefits.

You might think forensic psychiatrists would be more interested in serial killers than in mild-mannered employers. But don't be surprised if the employee/plaintiff asks a forensic psychiatrist to offer his or her opinion about whether, given the facts and circumstances of the case, you were biased or intended to discriminate. The psychiatrist may look at testimony from both sides, as well as your organization's characteristics, practices, and actions, before forming an opinion about discriminatory motives.

Employees most often use statistical evidence in disparate impact cases. The court can infer from the numbers that a seemingly neutral employment practice or policy actually has an unfavorable effect on members of a protected group.

The two kinds of numbers you need to worry about are population/work force statistics and pass/fail statistics. A plaintiff using population/work force statistics might attempt to show that blacks make up 20 percent of the labor force but only 2 percent of an organization's work force. Similarly, a plaintiff may use pass/fail statistics to show that only a small percentage of black or female employees pass a test or meet certain standards for promotion, compared with a large percentage of white or male workers who successfully pass that test or meet those standards.

WHAT'S THE DAMAGE?

Judges and juries are completely unpredictable. No matter how airtight a case you think you have, you may still lose. And when you lose, you usually have to open the corporate pocketbook to give the plaintiff damages, back pay, or both. Thus, it's important to know the type and extent of damages the law allows the employee/plaintiff to ask for.

Attorney's Fees

Under Title VII, the winner in a discrimination case can ask the loser to pay his or her attorney's fees. The ADEA does not explicitly provide for payment of attorney's fees as part of a judgment award to an employee, but the Fair Labor Standards Act does.

Attorneys are expensive, but there is, luckily, a cap on how much you'll be asked to pay if you lose a discrimination-related termination suit. The U.S. Supreme Court has held that an estimate of attorney's fees can be obtained by multiplying a *reasonable* number of hours spent on the case (it's up to the employee's attorney to keep accurate records of these hours) by an hourly rate based on the prevailing market rates for such services in the community.

The representation letter from an attorney to his or her employee client can take on added dimension here. The fees stated in the letter will probably put a ceiling on what you have to pay, because the rate an attorney actually charges a client is the rate on which the court must base its attorney's fee award.

Once the employee has won, he or she must file a *fee application*. The fee application should contain sufficiently detailed information about the hours logged and work done by the attorney. Also, some courts have specific rules regarding the time frame for making a fee application (usually, it must be done as soon as possible after the case is decided in the employee's favor).

If necessary, the judge may ask attorneys not connected with the case to testify about the value and quality of certain legal services. In general, however, there's no expert legal testimony in fee hearings because most judges are quite familiar with attorneys' fee structures and what constitutes quality legal work in a discrimination case.

Punitive Damages

As if attorney's fees and back pay weren't enough, you may also have to cough up a large sum in punitive damages to an ex-employee who wins a termination suit. As the name implies, punitive damages aim to "punish" an employer for doing something particularly offensive.

You're likely to be hit with punitive damages in wrongful discharge cases in which a termination goes against public policy. Examples include firing an employee because he or she has served on the jury for a lengthy trial and hasn't been able to come to work for several weeks; firing an employee who refuses to work in a nuclear facility that has been deemed unsafe; and firing an employee who won't use illegal methods to obtain information about the competition's product line.

These cases fall into the long-established judicial tradition of imposing punitive damages when one party unnecessarily harms or insults a vulnerable second party. Outrageous behavior by an employer that goes against a strong public interest or clearly defined individual right also warrants the imposition of punitive damages.

LESS PAIN, MORE GAIN

Two legal concepts you should be very interested in if you lose a termination case are "mitigation" and "offsets." Both are ways of reducing the amount of back wages and other damages that you will eventually have to pay.

Mitigation

Employees have a legal duty to mitigate (reduce) damages by looking for other work after being fired. In other words, your organization doesn't have to hemorrhage back pay while a fired employee jets off to the Caribbean.

But that doesn't mean the employee has to take the first job that comes along. The law won't compel a terminated worker go into another line of work, accept a demotion, or take a demeaning job. Most courts, however, require that after a period of looking for work without success, an employee should consider accepting suitable lower-paying employment to mitigate damages.

In general, employees cannot recover back pay from former employers for periods during which they were unable to work because of ill health, disability, or pregnancy.

Offsets

If the employee earns anything between being fired and receiving court-ordered back pay or damages, those interim earnings must be deducted from the amount of the final award. Such deductions are called *offsets*. The big problem with offsets, compared to mitigation, is that the courts can't seem to make up their minds about them.

For instance, the courts are up in the air as to whether unemployment benefits should be considered offsets. Some courts have held that unemployment benefits are collateral (sideline) earnings and cannot be deducted from back pay.

Workers' compensation might seem to be a different story: Under Title VII, the part of workers' comp meant to cover lost wages can be deducted from back pay. Again, though, there's not as much uniformity in how the courts deal with these sums as one might like.

When offsets favor employers, it's because the judge determines that the ex-employee would have not received unemployment or workers' comp benefits if he or she had not been illegally fired in the first place. So, unemployment or workers' comp received as a result of discriminatory firing must be deducted from the back pay award to prevent the ex-employee from getting a windfall.

Without doubt, employees and their smart lawyers can make life exceedingly difficult for you. In this chapter, I've described some of the nastiness they can hit you with; in the next, I'll look at employer-employee lawsuits from the other side— *your* side—and tell you how to fight back.

No matter how much hot water you get into, remember this:

Employers always have defenses and options in termination cases. Know what yours are—and use them!

CHAPTER 7

THE EMPLOYER'S COURT

When a competitor introduces a sizzling new product, you don't throw up your hands and sigh, "Well, XYZ, Inc., has taken over the market now. We may as well cash in our chips." And when corporate raiders start nibbling at your company, you don't offer them stock options. It doesn't matter who or what is challenging your corporate survival—you fight back!

Leaders of successful organizations probably learned how to fight back on the fifth-grade kickball field. They know that winners take charge; they're proactive rather than reactive. But when otherwise forceful and hard-driving managers become embroiled in termination lawsuits, this knowledge just seems to dissipate into the ether.

Many employers don't realize that the strategies that have helped them win in the business world can also help them win in the courtroom. In this chapter, I'll give you a game plan to assist you and your attorneys in dealing with a typical employment discrimination case. But you should be able to apply many of the same tactics if a fired employee slaps you with a wrongful discharge, defamation, or workers' compensation suit.

TAKE THE EEOC SERIOUSLY

After the settlement of their 15-year-old discrimination suit against a Texas-based military contractor, thousands of female employees and ex-employees are sharing $20 million in back pay—the largest settlement ever of a federal discrimination case against a single employer.

The case erupted when the contractor fired several female

workers, alleging that on-site exposure to chemicals could ruin their fertility or harm the children they might some day bear. Because of its solicitous (but not overly scientific) concern for female reproductive health, the company also decided to restrict hiring of women.

The female employees who brought the suit didn't have much trouble proving employment discrimination in federal court. To justify excluding female employees under such circumstances, said the judge, employers must supply "reputable objective scientific evidence" that a woman's exposure to a workplace hazard irretrievably harms potential offspring. They must also show that fetal damage results only when women are exposed to the hazard and that exposure doesn't affect male reproductive health.

In this case, the contracting company turned out to be its own worst enemy. When the women first filed their suit, the company laughed it off. Later, when the case went to trial, the company still considered it frivolous and not worthy of time, money, or legal muscle.

With its corporate pocketbook $20 million lighter, the contracting company now takes the case seriously. Unfortunately, it's a bit late.

Legal experts agree that the company lost partly because of its poor showing in the trial—a direct result of its lackadaisical attitude toward the case. Could the company have won with a more concerted effort? Perhaps not; this one's hard to call. Had it put up a good, tough fight and not automatically figured it couldn't lose, however, the company might have tipped the scales of justice in its favor.

As I explained in the last chapter, terminated employees often accuse their former employers of discrimination. The courts make employees jump through quite a few hoops to show that their discrimination claims are genuine, because a great many are transparent bluffs. A discrimination complaint filed with the Equal Employment Opportunity Commission (EEOC) is a great way to deflect attention from an employee's poor performance, and it makes the employee's former boss look like a combination of Simon Legree and Genghis Khan.

Employees have cried wolf about discrimination so often

that many employers have become cynical about EEOC complaints. That's not a good idea. You should *always* take such complaints seriously. Whether or not there's substance to them, they tend to take on a life of their own—and they can do you and your organization a lot of damage in the long run.

Early Warning Signs

When you receive an EEOC complaint from a terminated employee, the first thing you should do is review it for "hickeys"—errors, mishandled procedures, and discrepancies. Frequently, you can kill off a complaint in its infancy by determining that it doesn't meet all the requirements for a valid discrimination charge.

Most important is determining whether the EEOC has jurisdiction over your organization. At present, the EEOC's reach extends to all organizations employing 15 or more workers for 20 or more weeks in the current or preceding calendar year. The EEOC also has jurisdiction over state and local governments, most federal employees, and nonreligious educational institutions. If your company doesn't fall into any of these groups, the EEOC cannot prosecute you for employment discrimination—but don't think you're off the hook yet!

Also, the employee's charges must describe some type of discrimination that is actually against the law. For instance, an ex-employee can legitimately charge you with employment discrimination based on race, sex, religion, national origin, or age. But he or she cannot charge you with employment discrimination due to sexual preference, which is not under the EEOC's umbrella. (It is against the law in Massachusetts and a few other states.)

Moreover, the employee must file a charge with the EEOC within 180 days of the alleged discriminatory act, although the agency sometimes waives this period in unusual circumstances. Discipline and firing can involve a single isolated incident or an ongoing infraction of rules, so you might be able to use the 180-day rule to your advantage.

You'll want to find out for yourself whether discrimination

has indeed occurred and whether your company is under the gun legally. Begin by:

1. Reviewing the employee's personnel file, work record, and other written materials concerning the employee.
2. Interviewing the employee's supervisors and co-workers about incidents described in the EEOC charges.
3. Gathering facts and reports previously prepared in connection with the alleged discrimination.
4. Examining witness statements, in-house investigation reports, and the employee's statement from his or her former employers (if any).
5. Going over your personnel policies to determine whether the alleged discrimination represents a departure from what your organization has said and done in the past.

Make sure that you carefully consider the accuracy and reliability of your sources and that you weigh any mitigating circumstances that might help the employee's case.

A Measured Response

After receiving the employee's discrimination complaint, the EEOC will ask you to respond in writing to the charge. At this stage, it's vital that you get a clear account of your version of the facts into the record.

You must decide whether the response letter should come from your organization or your attorney. Go ahead and put the response on company letterhead if the outcome of the case boils down to whom the EEOC investigator chooses to believe. In such cases, showing that you have first-hand information about the facts of a discrimination charge makes you a more credible respondent. If the response consists primarily of legal analysis or argument, however, it will have more clout if your attorney signs it. No matter who generates and signs the letter, an attorney should always review a draft of it before anything hits the mail.

Thanks to the plaintiff's unusually broad discovery rights in discrimination cases (see the previous chapter), the EEOC will surely ask you to supply information, and lots of it. You must honor such requests, but that doesn't mean you have to give away the store! A bare-bones response is perfectly acceptable. To stay out of trouble, follow these guidelines:

1. Don't expand on the information you provide. Discuss only matters in the employee's complaint. For example, if an employee charges you with a discriminatory termination, don't start blabbing about hiring and promotions. Loose lips sink as many ships now as they did during World War II.

2. Never respond to questions from the EEOC that are clearly irrelevant to the allegations in the complaint. They're probably designed to fish around for other things to hit you with in court.

3. Don't hesitate to volunteer information that will present you in a positive light.

4. Don't submit signed affidavits or "sworn statements," and never attest to the validity or completeness of the documents you give the EEOC. Because you might have to amend or flesh out your responses later on, it's a good idea not to be pinned down to the information given in affidavits.

5. Don't rush your reply! You shouldn't feel pressured to meet tight deadlines; the EEOC investigator can easily arrange a continuance, and you should ask for one if you need it.

THE PLAYERS AND THEIR ROLES

Many employers and their attorneys are confused by EEOC investigations, beginning with who's supposed to do what. In fact, the EEOC investigator is the superstar who questions witnesses and others involved in the case; the employer's attorney is basically a spear carrier at this point.

Although investigators are supposed to be looking for "just the facts, ma'am," you should always keep in mind that EEOC investigators may not be as impartial as you might hope. An investigator is likely to decide a close call involving the facts of the case in the employee's favor.

Your attorney will have a lot to say later. In these early days, however, his or her role is limited to giving you advice and helping you deal with the other side's discovery ploys.

In his or her adjunct position, your counsel has no opportunity to speak officially or to examine or cross-examine witnesses during the investigation. But your attorney can use his or her knowledge of the case to help the EEOC investigator unravel the maze of the employee's complaint. For instance, the attorney can suggest questions for the investigator to pose to witnesses. (Naturally, the investigator will reject confusing or misleading questions.) And the attorney can also prepare your witnesses so that they don't make inconsistent or harmful statements.

Whoever your witnesses are, they should know how to act in an EEOC investigation. They must realize that the outcome of the investigation hinges on their credibility. Therefore, they should be civil to the investigator; they shouldn't get feisty and antagonize him or her. Likewise, they should never say that the complaining employee is lying. Such accusations usually end up rebounding on employers, making them seem unreasonable and belligerent.

AFTER THE INVESTIGATION

In an employment discrimination case, the EEOC investigation is merely the prologue. Depending on what the investigator digs up, the next step may be a settlement, dismissal of the discrimination charges, or a lawsuit.

Working It Out

The EEOC might informally encourage you to settle with the employee. Employer and employee can negotiate a settlement while the investigation is going on—but only before the EEOC makes its ruling.

You should settle only if:

1. Your defense is too full of holes to make it through a trial.
2. The complainant can easily back up his or her charges.

3. You don't have the resources to support expensive litigation.
4. You and the employee can achieve a settlement quickly, without spending a lot of money.
5. The settlement won't adversely affect other discrimination claims in the future.

Case Dismissed?

As mentioned earlier, many terminated employees use discrimination charges to retaliate against their former employers. The EEOC is pretty good at sniffing out phony discrimination claims, and if it finds no reasonable basis for a complaint, it will dismiss the charges.

But that's not necessarily the last you'll ever hear from your employee adversary and his or her complaint. Even if the EEOC chooses to drop the case, it will give the complainant a right-to-sue letter so that he or she can pursue the case without the EEOC's help.

If the employee opts to sue you, he or she must file the suit within 90 days of receiving the right-to-sue letter. Also, remember that the EEOC has only 180 days to take action after the filing of a discrimination charge. This time limit may lead the complainant to abandon the EEOC and demand a right-to-sue letter so that he or she can proceed directly against you.

Under the Age Discrimination in Employment Act (ADEA), the complaining employee does not need a right-to-sue letter to initiate a lawsuit against a former employer. But the employee must wait 60 days after filing a notice of intent to sue before filing the suit itself.

When the EEOC Goes to Court

The EEOC has the authority to sue an employer in federal court on behalf of a complainant (or, in a class action suit, complainants). The EEOC can file two types of suits: *enforcement actions,* which uphold the complainant's statutory rights, and *pattern-and-practice actions,* which uphold the federal antidiscrimination laws.

The EEOC won't bring an enforcement action until its attempts to get the employer and employee to conciliate their differences informally have run aground. Also, the EEOC cannot sue until at least 30 days after the employee has filed a discrimination charge. This 30-day minimum applies to deferrals from state agencies as well. In age discrimination cases, there's a 60-day minimum period before the EEOC can bring an enforcement action.

If the employee starts champing at the bit and decides to file his or her own suit in federal court, the EEOC won't duplicate effort by filing an enforcement action. The EEOC can still intervene in the employee's federal suit, though.

As far as practical concerns go, there's little difference between an EEOC enforcement action and a pattern-and-practice suit. For the EEOC to bring a pattern-and-practice suit, however, the U.S. attorney general's office must have a good reason to believe that an employer is "engaged in a pattern or practice of resistance" that denies employees their rights under Title VII or the ADEA.

Time and Time Again

In EEOC litigation, as in so many other things, time is the great leveler. You can use time to terrific advantage if you're ever the target of an EEOC action.

At first glance, it might seem as if time is definitely *not* on your side here. The time restrictions imposed on employees don't apply to the suits filed by the EEOC. For instance, the EEOC can file a pattern-and-practice suit on its own well beyond the 180-day period allowed for an employee to file charges against an employer. And the EEOC can sue an employer after the 90 days allowed for an individual to sue.

But you still have a way out: proving that the EEOC has dilly-dallied for no good reason and that this long, unexcused delay has hurt your organization severely. As long as you can show that the delay has caused you harm, the courts will probably bar the EEOC's suit. Keep in mind, though, that it's not enough to say that you've been hurt only because a lot of time has passed.

STRIKE FIRST, STRIKE HARD

Too many employers lose termination cases because they sit on their hands. At the beginning of this chapter, I talked about some gut-level basics of business success that are just as applicable to fighting employment lawsuits. Perhaps the most critical of these is the need to be proactive, not reactive. You never want to relinquish control of the suit to the employee. Always take the initiative!

Start by trying to knock the employee's case out of the ring as early as possible. Begin by reviewing the complaint to ensure that the employee/plaintiff filed a charge with the EEOC within the requisite period; that the plaintiff received a right-to-sue letter; and that the plaintiff is claiming that you did something that can and should be dealt with in court.

Also, take a look at the type of relief (back pay, damages, and so on) the plaintiff is asking for, and determine whether it's allowed by the law the plaintiff is accusing you of violating. The kind of relief available to the plaintiff varies from statute to statute.

Under quite a few laws, you may have to pay the employee's legal fees if he or she wins the case (see Table 7–1). Title VII permits an employee fired for discriminatory reasons to ask for back pay (or, if necessary, front pay), attorney's fees, and reinstatement in his or her job. The employee can also request that the judge issue an injunction against future discriminatory actions by your organization. The slim piece of good news is that the employee cannot ask you to pay damages of any kind.

Along with injunctions, reinstatement, back pay and front pay, and attorney's fees, the ADEA also allows employees to request payment of liquidated damages. It does not permit punitive or "pain and suffering" damages, unless the employer has intentionally and recklessly discriminated on the basis of age.

If the complaint is defective, or if the plaintiff is asking for some kind of relief not allowed under existing law, you and your attorneys should make tracks to get the complaint dismissed as quickly as possible.

TABLE 7-1
Laws Awarding Attorney's Fees to Employees Who Win Suits

Age Discrimination in Employment Act
Americans with Disabilities Act of 1990
Civil Rights Act of 1964, Title II, 42 U.S.C. 2000a-3(b)
Civil Rights Act of 1964, Title III, 42 U.S.C. 2000b-1
Civil Rights Act of 1964, Title VII, 42 U.S.C. 2000e-5(k)*
Civil Rights Attorney's Fees Awards Act of 1976, 42 U.S.C. 1988
Civil Service Reform Act of 1978, 5 U.S.C. 5596(b) and 7701(g)
Clean Air Act, 42 U.S.C. 7413(b), 7604(d), and 7606(f)
Consumer Product Safety Act, 15 U.S.C. 2059(e)(4) and 2060(c)
Ethics in Government Act, 2 U.S.C. 288i(d)
Freedom of Information Act, 5 U.S.C. 552(a) (4) (E)
Government in the Sunshine Act, 5 U.S.C. 522b(1)
Noise Control Act, 42 U.S.C. 4911(d)
Privacy Act, 5 U.S.C. 552a(g) (3) (B) and 552a(g) (4)
Privacy Protection Act of 1980, 42 U.S.C. 2000aa-6
Rehabilitation Act of 1973, 29 U.S.C. 794a
Right to Financial Privacy Act of 1978, 12 U.S.C. 3417(a) and 3418
Toxic Substances Control Act, 15 U.S.C. 2618(d), 2619(c) (2), and 2620(b)
   (4) (C)

* Under Title VII, the "prevailing party" can recover costs, including attorney's fees. But it is more difficult for a winning employer to collect attorney's fees from a losing plaintiff than vice versa.

Technical Brilliance

When sucker-punching an employee's lawsuit early in the game doesn't knock it off its feet, you and your counsel can try to have the suit dismissed on technical grounds.

If the 90-day limit on filing charges is ignored, an employee loses his or her right to prosecute a lawsuit. You shouldn't have trouble getting a Title VII suit dismissed if the plaintiff files the action 11 months after receiving right-to-sue notification from the EEOC. Unless there are extraordinary circumstances, lack of timely prosecution is a legitimate basis for dismissal. You must show, however, that the failure to prosecute was solely the result of the plaintiff's laziness.

Sometimes plaintiffs engage in a lot of hand waving in court; they present opinions but no real facts. Without facts, the plaintiff can't demonstrate discrimination, and without proof of discrimination, he or she certainly can't ask for back pay or damages. In such situations, it's appropriate for your attorneys to make a motion to have the case dismissed. Unfortunately, these motions are difficult to sustain because the courts interpret Title VII and ADEA complaints so liberally. As I've noted, discrimination is tough to prove, so the courts will give plaintiffs more leeway than they might otherwise have.

A motion to dismiss might also be appropriate if the employee's complaint is vague and doesn't give specifics to which you can respond. And a motion to halt proceedings in court is certainly the right course when you and the employee decide to try one more time to resolve your differences through reconciliation.

YOUR DEFENSIVE LINE

Despite your lawyers' fancy footwork, the employee's case may survive unscathed and go to trial. That means you'll have to come up with a defense. Naturally, you want a strong, concerted defense that gives you a reasonable shot at winning.

In discrimination rulings, the courts have recognized several defenses for employer behavior that might otherwise appear discriminatory. You should be able to extend these defenses to wrongful discharge and defamation cases, many of which are rooted in discrimination charges.

Legitimate Objective

The court will excuse seemingly discriminatory actions if you can produce evidence that they serve a *legitimate employment objective*. You no longer have to prove that the actions were a matter of "business necessity." That's to your advantage: Business necessity is notoriously hard to demonstrate. You must show that there was a compelling need to make a decision out of business necessity, that your business would have fallen apart had you not made the decision, and that there was no reasonable alternative.

Bona Fide Occupational Qualification

Employers often invoke the bona fide occupational qualification (BFOQ) defense in sex discrimination cases. It's something like the business necessity defense, because it states that treating members of a protected group differently is "reasonably necessary to the normal operation of a particular business or enterprise."

The concept of business necessity grew out of judicial proceedings, but Title VII actually provides for the BFOQ defense. The courts have also expanded the BFOQ to apply to age discrimination cases brought under the ADEA.

Usually, however, the courts interpret the BFOQ very narrowly. For example, they've upheld the use of the BFOQ defense to support an employer's prohibition against hiring women for contact positions at an all-male prison. But they've rejected the notion that customer preference should determine who gets hired and fired. No matter how many male business travelers want to be waited on by young female flight attendants, airlines can't claim that being a young woman is a BFOQ for the job.

Some of the major commercial airlines have fired flight attendants, especially older ones, for being "overweight." The courts have struck down weight limits that affected only women and that were established because customers like their flight attendants slim. But the courts have upheld weight standards that apply equally to male and female flight attendants.

Bona Fide Seniority Systems

The U.S. Supreme Court has rejected the claim that seniority systems tend to perpetuate discrimination. That certainly puts the stamp of approval on using seniority as a defense in an employment discrimination suit.

An employment practice that may ultimately discriminate against older workers or other protected groups is OK if it involves a bona fide seniority system. In other words, you can have different pay scales or employment conditions based on seniority, and you can award more privileges to senior workers. Remember, though, that the seniority system must be genuine; it can't be a front for other kinds of discrimination that *are* against the law.

Religious Exemptions

You may think that Title VII's ban on religious discrimination in employment is about as ironclad as they come. In fact, Title VII contains exemptions that let religious organizations use religion as a factor in hiring, promoting, and terminating employees— and as a defense in discrimination suits.

A parochial school run by a Catholic diocese, for instance, has the right to hire only Catholic teachers, if that's what it wants to do. In general, a religious institution can restrict its personnel to members of a particular religion if the institution is wholly or partially owned, supported, or controlled by that religious group.

There is a catch, though. To invoke the Title VII exemptions in court, you must be an actual religious corporation, association, or society. Under the law, a children's home affiliated with, say, the Baptist Church is not a true religious corporation. If the home tries to use Title VII exemptions to defend its firing of all non-Baptist employees, it will surely wash out in court.

GET THE INFO EARLY

In a lawsuit, information is more precious than rubies. The side that wins a discrimination case is usually the side that's fastest on its feet in obtaining useful information. Once litigation begins, both sides have access to each other's records and other pertinent material.

The earlier you exercise your discovery rights, the better off you'll be. What you discover will tell you a lot about the direction and strength of the plaintiff's case. You'll also keep the plaintiff and his or her lawyers busy—and out of your hair. Finally, if you require the plaintiff to respond to your discovery inquiries at an early stage, you may force him or her to give answers on the fly.

Answers that aren't well thought out may eventually cause the plaintiff to tone down his or her claims as the case progresses.

Here's what you should do to make your discovery process a fruitful one:

- Schedule the plaintiff's depositions as soon as possible.
- Inspect documents in the EEOC files. Although this information isn't available to the public, it is open to both you and the plaintiff. (You may not be able to gain access to file documents concerning informal conciliation efforts by an EEOC investigator.)
- If an EEOC computer expert includes your records in an on-line database, you have the right to examine the database code, the media on which it is stored, and even its user manual.
- Use interrogatories (written requests) and motions for the production of documents to get a definitive statement from the other side about the alleged discrimination. The plaintiff's responses will help you determine what the case is about and, more important, what it's not about.

The Fine Art of Depositions

Most employment discrimination complaints are just boilerplate allegations with the name of an employer typed in. Don't be surprised if the complaint states that you committed every kind of discrimination under the sun and violated the civil rights of every protected group the plaintiff belongs to.

Depositions are a powerful tool for culling out the facts from the boilerplate. During a deposition, an employee may break down and admit that some of the statements in his or her complaint fall a little short of the truth.

To obtain factual admissions, you and your lawyers don't have to menace the employee with a spotlight and a syringe of Pentathol. There are plenty of perfectly legitimate ways to extract honest answers in an employee deposition:

1. Get the plaintiff to identify the practices and policies that he or she believes are discriminatory.
2. Ask the plaintiff to list every discriminatory action he or

she personally experienced, as well as all the discriminatory incidents that he or she is aware of.
3. Lead the plaintiff through each allegation in the complaint.
4. Ask the plaintiff to confirm aspects of your business that
can help you build a business necessity defense. (Frequently, the plaintiff's attorney will draft an employment discrimination complaint without knowing the specifics of the employer's business!)
5. Obtain admissions against co-plaintiffs, if any. The employee may say something that helps his or her case and
damages a co-plaintiff's case.

You and your attorneys may also have to obtain depositions
from the other side's expert witnesses. Many plaintiffs use statistics to demonstrate discrimination. It doesn't hurt to quiz the
plaintiff's statistical guru about the methods used to develop the
statistical evidence.

Off-Limits to Employees

The employee and his or her lawyers will attempt to pry as much
information out of you as their discovery rights permit. Keep in
mind, though, that they don't have carte blanche. The information they're seeking must be relevant to the case; they can't go on
a fishing expedition in your company's private files. Likewise,
their request for information must be specifically limited to the
issues involved in the case.

The employee's attorney may think that asking for the same
things twice is pretty clever. The judge is likely to think that it's
a bonehead play, and will probably tell you that you're under no
obligation to go along with either request.

Most courts will protect your affirmative action program
information because it's considered confidential. Employers compile and disclose such information to the government to comply
with Title VII and Executive Order 11246. The public policy
behind these requirements mandates "frank self-criticism and
evaluation" by employers. Giving employees access to such information would put a damper on this kind of honest self-appraisal.

PROSECUTE VIGOROUSLY

You've probably heard the old saw about the prosecution having the burden of proof. Don't think this means your side doesn't have to work hard to present its case!

Whether a trial involves a speeding ticket or an antidiscrimination beef, the winner is the one whom the judge or jury believes. The right kind of evidence will bolster your credibility and help put you in the winner's circle.

In Title VII actions, for instance, the Supreme Court has ruled that statistical evidence is no longer enough to prove disparate impact. The plaintiff who wants to prove that there are more minority group members than whites in low-level jobs at a cannery must point to specific employer practices that affect employment opportunities for whites and nonwhites. Likewise, in age discrimination cases brought under the ADEA, counsel must prove that an employee would not have been let go had he or she not been past a certain "prime" age.

Once the plaintiff establishes his or her case, you must produce evidence of a legitimate business or employment objective for the alleged discriminatory action. Because the burden of *persuasion* rests with the plaintiff, however, you don't actually have to convince the judge or jury to accept that objective; all you have to do is offer some evidence that it exists. It's up to the plaintiff's attorneys to persuade the court that your business or employment objective is anything but legitimate.

Your side does have the burden of proof when an employee establishes that an employer's decision to hire, fire, or promote an employee involved a "discriminatory element." The employer must prove that he or she would have done the same thing even if the discriminatory element had not been present.

Let's say that you decide to fire Betsy L., one of the few African-Americans working for your company. Betsy is an executive secretary with fine skills and many years of experience. Nonetheless, you think she's burning out; she's made some expensive mistakes and has called in sick at least six or seven days a month for the past half-year. You've counseled and warned her, but nothing has changed.

As it happens, there's a discreet move among some firms in your town to discourage employing blacks in high-visibility positions. Naturally, Betsy knows about this unwritten discriminatory policy—and naturally, she's going to accuse your company of going along with it.

If you want to win the suit, the ball will be in your court. You'll have to come up with a preponderance of evidence showing that Betsy's performance was going downhill and that you would have fired her from her high-visibility job regardless of the highly illegal covert discrimination practiced by other companies. You may also have to provide employee manuals and other evidence showing that your company does not approve of any form of discrimination.

WATCH OUT FOR WITNESSES

The evidence you put before the court will probably come from witnesses—eyewitnesses, expert witnesses, and others. A charismatic witness can sway a jury and sometimes even a judge. A colorless witness can lose a case, no matter how knowledgeable he or she is. And a witness who seems not to be clear on the concept does you no good at all.

Your witnesses should be close to the issue and familiar with the employee's performance and job history with your organization, as well as your defense strategies. Also, if your human resources staffers testify, they should know your company's policies and day-to-day employment practices like their own names.

Expert witnesses in termination cases may include statisticians to make work force comparisons and analyze the plaintiff's numbers; physicians to testify in cases involving BFOQs and whether illness or injury affects an employee's ability to do a job; and industrial engineers to analyze physical requirements for job performance, compare job duties in equal-pay cases, and perform necessary business analysis. Whoever they are, your expert witnesses should be personable, and their testimony should be simple, concise, and convincing.

Block Those Statistics

The employee will probably use statistics to determine the percentage of available female or minority group members in the relevant labor market and to compare that figure with the number of women or minority group members you employ. For instance, a terminated female employee may come up with statistics (which are, of course, superbly amenable to manipulation) showing that women represent more than half the work force, yet hold only a tiny portion of managerial slots in your organizational hierarchy. The employee might then use these statistics to prove that sexism is halting the upward march of women at your company.

Typically, employee statistics paint your entire work force as a single, homogeneous body. To blunt statistical attacks, you must show that no work force is as unilateral as that depicted by the plaintiff. Emphasize the differences between available labor markets for, say, accounting, management, warehouse and shipping workers, and production employees.

It's been said that employees do so well in discrimination cases because they know how to use the antidiscrimination laws to their advantage. But it doesn't have to be that way!

If a terminated employee goes to the EEOC and charges you with discrimination, you should have a good chance of doing well in court if you remember these things:

Investigate facts carefully, obtain information early, and press your defense aggressively.

CHAPTER 8

THE PINK SLIP BLUES

You have control over the who, how, and why of termination for cause. Employees even have control over whether they get fired: Usually, all they have to do is improve their performance or stop breaking your organization's rules.

But layoffs are another story. It's impossible to predict how the economic winds will blow. When there are mass plant closings in an industry, or when unbridled mergers and acquisitions send entire divisions to the unemployment line, everyone ends up in a daze.

Many managers handle layoffs badly. They might not realize that there are right and wrong ways to lay off workers, or they might be too upset and confused to care. What do you think happens in such situations? Often, the laid-off workers take their anger and frustration straight to a lawyer's office or federal agency.

Now, suing a company in such bad financial straits that it has to lay off workers may seem like the ultimate insult added to injury. But workers do it all the time. As the *Boston Globe* said in a recent article on firing-related litigation, "It isn't easy to fire a worker, even if business is bad."

When several dozen employees got pink slips after a high-tech service firm won a big government contract to install computers, the employees claimed that the company was using the contract as an excuse to squeeze them out of their jobs. The company argued that the contract would last only two years, and that much more was needed to bail it out of its financial doldrums. The employees were not impressed with this hard-luck story: They slapped a $100 million lawsuit on the firm.

Although some unscrupulous companies use layoffs as a

means of getting rid of troublesome employees who can't legally be fired for cause, no one wants to lay off trusted and valuable workers. Unfortunately, you have no way of knowing whether there will be an economic slowdown or even a recession, whether your industry will be undermined by foreign competition or defense spending cuts, or whether a corporate shark will gobble up your business. As a result, you have no way of knowing whether there will be a major layoff or even a shutdown in your company's future.

The law on plant closings and layoffs is fairly young, and it's changing all the time. That's all the more reason for you to understand and monitor it.

FAIR WARNING

The principal law regulating how employers should handle facility closings is the federal Worker Adjustment and Retraining Notification Act (WARN). You may remember the congressional brouhaha over this act, which started life as the so-called 60-Day Plant Closing Bill in the mid-1980s. In its present state, however, WARN is a big gun only for big companies: It applies to employers with 100 or more full-time employees or whose entire work force puts in at least 4,000 non-overtime hours per week.

WARN is an apt acronym for this law, which requires employers to give 60 days' warning about closings or mass layoffs to an employee representative or to each affected employee, to the state dislocated worker unit, and to the chief elected official of the city, county, or other local government unit where the closing or layoff will take place.

To understand how WARN works, some definitions are in order. A "mass layoff" is a reduction in force that does not result from a plant closing, and that causes at least one third of the full-time employees at a single site to lose their jobs. An "affected employee" is one who is likely to lose his or her job because of a layoff lasting more than six months, or whose work hours will be cut by at least half during each month of a six-month period.

You definitely don't want to run afoul of WARN's requirements to give notice of closings and layoffs to affected employees.

Violators may have to give back pay and benefits to the affected employees for the period of the violation, up to 60 days. Worse, you may have to pay an additional $500 in civil penalties if you "forget" to tell a local government official about the closing or layoff.

Although WARN doesn't authorize the courts to issue injunctions against plant closings or layoffs if affected employees win a suit, it does allow them to collect attorney's fees from you. It also gives affected employees the right to sue you on their own, but only in federal court.

WARN does not take precedence over rights guaranteed by a contract or another statute. If a union contract or a federal or state law requires, say, a 90-day warning period, you must give affected employees at least 90 days' notice of the closing or layoff.

If you get into trouble under WARN for failing to notify your employees about plans to shut down operations or carry out mass layoffs, one of these defenses may save you:

1. The company was sold, and the obligation to give notice to the employees fell to the purchaser after the effective date of the sale.
2. You offered to transfer the affected employees to a different job site, within reasonable commuting distance and with no more than a six-month break in service, or to any company location, regardless of distance, with no more than a six-month break in service. (For this defense to fly, the employees must have accepted within 30 days of the offer, closing, or layoff, whichever came last.)
3. The closing or layoff occurred because a short-term project or assignment ended, and the employees knew that their employment was finite when they were hired.
4. The closing or layoff occurred because of a strike or lockout.
5. You were actively seeking capital or business for a faltering company that would have helped prevent or at least postpone the shutdown, and you honestly believed that giving notice of a closing would have hurt your chances of obtaining the capital or business.

6. The closing or layoff occurred because of business circumstances that no one could reasonably foresee.
7. The closing or layoff occurred because of a natural disaster.

UNDERHANDED LAYOFFS

John L., a bond sales manager at a financially squeezed investment brokerage, is told to lay off five employees. After axing two new hires, John immediately fingers two of the less spectacular performers in the bond division, Stan T. and Anna S. Both have met their sales quotas, but barely. John also decides to can Claudio C., the scion of a wealthy Argentinian family. Claudio put together one of the biggest deals in the firm's history, but John considers him a spoiled rich kid who spends too much time at his tailor and the racetrack, and not enough at the office. "I'll be happy to see the last of these losers," smiles John as he sends his hit list to Human Resources for processing.

When Stan, Anna, and Claudio sue for wrongful discharge, John learns how quickly "losers" can become big winners. The judge rules that John erred in using subjective criteria such as performance and quality as decision-making parameters for laying off workers. Stan, Anna, and Claudio each receive $50,000 plus attorney's fees.

Too many employers try to stretch a legitimate layoff so that they can weed out employees who haven't done anything to get fired, but who nonetheless are thorns in the company's side. The result, as you might imagine, is a locustlike swarm of lawsuits.

When you're targeting employees for layoffs, it's best to rely on completely objective criteria, such as length of employment or good old business necessity. Performance is a rotten yardstick for determining who should be laid off; it's too volatile and open to interpretation.

If you really want a one-way ticket to court, try using layoffs to avoid paying pensions or benefits to a qualified employee, or to punish a worker who's missed a lot of work to serve on a jury.

Pension Penalties

Some companies think that they can save a few dollars by laying off workers who are close to being vested in a company pension plan or who have accumulated substantial benefits. Wrong move! Such actions directly violate the Employee Retirement Income Security Act (ERISA), which covers pension and welfare benefit plans. Under ERISA, welfare benefit plans include health insurance, disability and sick pay, and unemployment insurance, but not routine vacation pay.

The act applies to plans established or maintained by employers "in commerce," or by organizations representing employees of qualified employers. The act excludes government and church plans.

Here are ERISA's prime directives:

1. You must meet minimum vesting, funding, fiduciary, reporting, and disclosure requirements for all applicable pension plans. (These requirements do not apply to welfare benefit plans.)
2. You do not have laissez-faire in imposing participation requirements for applicable plans.
3. You must count *all* employee service with your organization toward employees' pension.

An amendment to ERISA states that you must give employees and their beneficiaries an opportunity to retain company health insurance coverage at the group rate for 18 months after "qualifying events." For example, if a covered employee was laid off or terminated for anything except gross misconduct, he or she would be able to hang on to his or her health insurance at the group rate. Likewise, if the employee died, his or her dependents would have the option of picking up the coverage at the group rate.

It is illegal to lay off or fire employees for exercising their rights under ERISA, or to interfere with those rights. You're in trouble if employees realize that you're making a practice of laying off workers who are on the verge of vestiture in the company pension plan.

The Internal Revenue Service administers ERISA's participation, vesting, and funding requirements; the Department of Labor handles its fiduciary, reporting, and disclosure requirements. The Department of Labor has the authority to investigate all possible ERISA violations, and to sue in federal court as it deems necessary. Employees and their beneficiaries can also bring private suits against employers who trample on their ERISA rights. So, if you think layoffs are a nice, neat way to cut down on pension or benefit payments, think again: You could find yourself in the midst of both a government investigation *and* a private lawsuit.

Jury Duties

Carole P. gets called to sit on the jury for a complex murder trial. About three weeks into the trial, the judge decides to sequester the jury. The trial goes on for four months; it looks as if it may go on forever. During this time, the company asks you to lay off several workers in Carole's department. You figure that Carole hasn't been around for so long that she may as well be gone anyway, so you lay her off in absentia. The trial ends shortly after the layoff. Carole, incensed that she has no job to return to, sues you.

Sometimes it's hard to predict how a hypothetical case will turn out in court. This one, however, is easy: You don't have a prayer of making Carole's termination stick.

Federal law states that you cannot dismiss, intimidate, or coerce employees who are called to serve on federal juries. If an employee needs to stay out of work to meet this civic obligation, you must treat the time off as a leave of absence.

Employees who get laid off or fired because of their jury service have the right to sue their ex-employers in federal district court. A winning employee can demand reinstatement in his or her former job with full seniority, damages for loss of wages and benefits, and attorney's fees if he or she has to hire a private attorney. (That may not be necessary, as the court will provide the employee with counsel if desired.)

State law also prevents you from laying off, firing, or otherwise discriminating against an employee asked to serve on a jury or to testify in a trial. Moreover, you cannot demand that the employee use up vacation or sick leave if he or she must go to court for these reasons. Although violating state jury-service statutes may not seem serious (it's a misdemeanor in many jurisdictions), it's still not a great idea.

Citizens and Aliens

Congress passed the Immigration Reform and Control Act (IRCA) in 1986, mostly to stem the flood tide of illegal aliens spilling across the southern borders of the United States. According to a General Accounting Office (GAO) report, IRCA has fueled widespread discriminatory layoffs.

The GAO report states that many employers have laid off or fired foreign nationals because the law does not provide a simple or reliable way to verify employees' legal right to work. Fearing crackdowns by the Immigration and Naturalization Service, employers are using layoffs and phony facility closings to get rid of foreign-born "problem" employees.

That is not the intention of IRCA, which applies to all private and government organizations with more than three employees. IRCA actually prohibits employers from using national origin or citizenship status as grounds for firing, laying off, or refusing to hire qualified foreign nationals (other than illegal aliens, of course). Its provisions regarding discrimination based on national origin do not extend to employers already covered by Title VII of the Civil Rights Act.

IRCA protects legally registered aliens who plan to become citizens. Occasionally, however, national security laws or the requirements of doing business with government organizations may demand that you hire or retain only U.S. citizens. In such instances, you cannot be accused of discriminating against legal aliens because of their citizenship status.

Although IRCA forbids discrimination based on national origin, it doesn't overtly stop you if you wish to hire a citizen instead of an alien. The act is much clearer on the subject of layoffs: When a citizen and an alien are equally qualified, the law lets you lay off the alien first.

The Office of Special Counsel for Immigration-Related Unfair Employment Practices investigates IRCA discrimination complaints. An employee must file charges with the agency within 180 days of the alleged discriminatory act. The Special Counsel's investigation can last up to 120 days. Then the employee has 90 days to bring a private administrative action against the employer.

Workers' Comp Woes

State laws prohibit you from laying off an employee who files a workers' compensation claim or who is about to testify in workers' comp proceedings. An employee laid off for these reasons can sue in state court for an injunction against your company, as well as for damages, attorney's fees, back pay, and reinstatement in his or her former job.

When an employee has been out of work for a long time because of a work-related injury, some companies get the not-so-bright idea of targeting him or her for a layoff. (It's the same rationale as that for laying off a worker serving on a jury for a lengthy trial: "So-and-So hasn't been around in such a long time that we may as well make it official.") Other companies try to say that the employee has missed so much work that he or she can be fired for absenteeism.

Both moves are blatantly illegal. Absences due to work-related injuries can't be tallied as infractions of your company's absenteeism policy unless the absences exceed six months or your organization's circumstances have changed so greatly that there's no alternative to laying off or firing the injured employee.

An Honest Day's Work

Better known as the minimum wage law, the Fair Labor Standards Act (FLSA) states that you cannot lay off employees because you don't want to give them the legal minimum hourly wage or overtime pay.

The FLSA applies to all employees working in interstate commerce, to government workers, and to all employers with two or more workers. It doesn't cover executives, administrative and professional employees, or outside salespersons.

The Department of Labor, which administers the FLSA, investigates complaints and inspects companies for violations. The department can sue in federal court, or employees can bring a federal suit of their own.

Losing any suit is unpleasant, but losing an FLSA suit can put an especially big dent in your corporate finances. You may have to give the employee up to two years of unpaid minimum wages or overtime (three years if the violation is deemed "willful"), plus the same amount in damages. An employee laid off for exercising his or her rights under the law would also be entitled to reinstatement, back pay, and damages.

Executive Orders

Employers who do business with the federal government must toe the line on discrimination in hiring and firing. As you might expect, the government also frowns on discriminatory layoffs.

Here are the key executive orders that employees might invoke in alleging a discriminatory layoff or dismissal prompted by a plant closing:

1. Executive Orders 11246 and 11375 forbid federal contractors with contracts of $10,000 or more from discriminating against employees on the basis of race, sex, religion, color, or national origin. (Contract amounts can be lumped together for a 12-month period.)
2. Executive Order 11141 forbids federal contractors with contracts of $10,000 or more per year from discriminating on the basis of age.
3. Executive Order 11914 prohibits discrimination against handicapped individuals in federally assisted programs.

The Office of Federal Contract Compliance Programs (OFCCP) administers these executive orders. The OFCCP processes individual complaints and can also initiate enforcement actions. An employee must file a complaint with the agency within 180 days of the alleged discriminatory act. If the OFCCP prosecutes and wins, the court might issue an injunction against the contractor and award the employee back pay. It might even suspend or terminate the employer's contract.

UNION DUES

Several employees of a magazine publishing company decide that it's time to form a union. They meet with the rep from a large national union, who encourages them to organize. Most of the union activity involves the art, production, and typesetting departments; out of fear or other reasons, the editorial and business staff keep their distance.

Eventually Al F., the company president, gets wind of the union effort and lays off almost everyone in the art and typesetting departments. In the production department, however, he makes a fatal mistake: He lays off Neil B., a production assistant who had been an active organizer and a "troublemaker," but not two other production workers who had had nothing to do with the union drive. Neil and some of the other laid-off workers head straight for the National Labor Relations Board (NLRB). It doesn't take long for yet another lawsuit to start lurching through the courts.

Had Al been on the ball, he would have known that the National Labor Relations Act (NLRA) protects the rights of workers to organize labor unions and to engage in collective bargaining. It also prohibits employers from laying off workers because they are union members or because they agree with union goals. The message is simple: You can't use layoffs to hide a purge of union workers or sympathizers. (On the other hand, you can't lay off workers because they choose *not* to take part in union activities.)

The NLRA applies to all private nonagricultural employers involved in interstate commerce. To be affected by the act, a retail or service organization must have a gross business volume of more than $500,000 with some interstate commerce activity. Nonretail businesses must furnish $50,000 in goods or services to firms in or out of state, or must purchase and receive $50,000 in goods or services directly from firms outside the state or from an in-state seller of goods or services originating outside the state.

The NLRA's reach also extends to nonprofit institutions and to some organizations sponsored by religious groups, such as secular colleges with denominational ties. No matter how noble their intent, such institutions can be prosecuted if they lay off workers or close facilities to lock out a union.

Responsibility for prosecution rests with the NLRB, an independent federal agency with headquarters in Washington, D.C., and regional offices nationwide. In enforcing the NLRA, the NLRB's goal is to ensure that employees hang on to their rights to form, join, and assist labor organizations. The NLRB polices the act to keep employers from coercing or threatening union workers and sympathizers, and from interfering with their NLRA-guaranteed rights.

Employees who believe that an employer has stomped on their union rights must file an unfair labor charge with the NLRB within six months of the layoff or other alleged violation of the NLRA. The board investigates the charge and decides whether to issue a complaint against the employer. The NLRB's general counsel tries complaints before an administrative law judge, with appeals to the full five-member board in Washington, D.C., and then to the appropriate federal Court of Appeals.

In determining whether employees' union activities are at the root of layoffs or firings, the NLRB looks at these factors:

1. The timing of the layoff or firing in relation to the employees' union activities.
2. The reason given for the layoff or firing.
3. The employer's knowledge of the union activity.
4. The employer's feelings about the union activity; whether there is a strong antiunion bias in the company's managerial ranks.
5. Disparate treatment of the laid-off or fired union members.
6. Departure from the company's established rules and procedures in dealing with union members.
7. Failure to warn union members or sympathizers about impending layoffs.
8. Other possible reasons for the layoffs or firings.

The NLRA is a remedial rather than a punitive statute: It is not designed to sanction anti-union employers, but to help employees regain what they've lost as a result of union activities. The NLRB or the judge might demand that an employer give a laid-off employee back pay and benefits, and reinstate him or her in the same or an equivalent job. But the employer doesn't have to worry about injunctions and damages.

By the way, the NLRA doesn't just take potshots at employers. Labor unions can also come under fire if they compel an employer to lay off employees they don't like, or if they picket or apply economic pressure to get an employer to lay off certain employees or shut down nonunion shops.

Working on the Railroad

The NLRA isn't the only law that safeguards the rights of employees to unionize. Some industries bolster its protection with their own laws. For instance, the Railway Labor Act (RLA) gives railroad and airline workers the right to organize and bargain collectively, and to choose a representative for bargaining without interference, influence, or coercion.

Two agencies are responsible for working things out between railroads or airlines and their unions. The National Railroad Adjustment Board resolves disputes. The National Mediation Board assists in negotiations between carriers and unions, and conducts elections to determine union representation.

Railroad and airline workers can sue their employers in federal court. Employers found guilty of deliberately violating the RLA by laying off union workers may be subject to penalties.

SMOOTH LAYOFFS

XYZ, Inc., has just merged with Foobaron International. Foobaron thinks there's too much dead wood on XYZ's staff and demands that XYZ's management lay off 33 percent of its work force before the merger becomes final. XYZ has never laid off workers before, and it's not sure how to proceed. Roger E., the president of XYZ, tells the company's managers and supervisors to "do the right thing," whatever that may be. So, Helen N. uses performance to thin out the ranks, Ralph F. goes by seniority, and Ken Y. asks for volunteers. It doesn't take long for the lawsuits to start pouring in.

XYZ got caught short because it had no guidelines to help Helen, Ralph, and Ken apply the same standards to all layoffs. A layoff and shutdown policy would have muted the likelihood of XYZ being charged with discrimination or labor law violations.

Don't let this happen to you! When mergers, buyouts, or business problems force you to cut your work force or close a facility, have a clearcut policy and make sure that managers stick to it.

In developing your layoff and shutdown policy, keep these points in mind:

1. Put the policy in writing, *before* a mass layoff or plant closing occurs.
2. Select certain managers to be responsible for ensuring that the policy is followed uniformly by all other managers and supervisors.
3. Give affected employees written notice of a layoff or plant closing.
4. Offer counseling to employees who are having trouble dealing with a layoff or shutdown.
5. Always document an attempt to help an employee before a layoff, and place the writeup in the employee's personnel file.
6. Meet with employees to explain how the layoff or shutdown will be carried out and to clear up misunderstandings. Ensuring that employees know the full story will help ease tensions.
7. Make sure that a layoff or shutdown does not appear to retaliate against union members or other employees who are just exercising their legal rights, and that it does not appear to discriminate against members of protected groups.
8. Do not describe a layoff or plant closing as a "termination" in personnel or other records. Put down the employee's last workday as the date of separation.
9. Base severance pay for laid-off workers on length of service and level of responsibility, not on performance. Always obtain approval to award severance pay before promising it to employees.
10. Pay laid-off workers in full, as mandated by state labor laws.
11. Notify company personnel before a laid-off employee's last workday about whether the employee has received a

cash advance or other company property that must be returned.

12. Give laid-off employees priority consideration over new applicants for future job openings.

Supervisors are responsible for ensuring that everyone follows these policies, but your company's human resources department should handle the administrative aspects of layoffs and shutdowns. To safeguard everyone's rights, coordinate with the human resources department as early as possible before the proposed layoff date.

Usually, employees' life and health insurance coverage ends on the last day of the month in which the employee is laid off. Under the federal COBRA requirements, however, laid-off employees have the option of continuing the coverage by paying group rates for up to 18 months after the layoff.

From Pink Slips to Rehiring

Levels of employment in seasonal industries such as agriculture and economically unstable industries such as aerospace tend to ebb and flow. In response, many companies with varying or cyclical employment needs have developed policies so that they can lay off and then recall workers as necessary.

As you might expect, such policies can be legal dynamite. If you need one for your company, make sure it includes the following elements:

1. A specific statement that the recall/rehire policy is not a contractual right and that you are free to deviate from it or eliminate it at any time.

2. A notice statement declaring that if the employee wishes to be considered for recall or rehire, he or she must contact you periodically and must provide you with his or her current address and phone number.

3. A policy statement that all recall and rehire decisions will be based on qualifications and experience.

4. A time limit on giving laid-off employees priority for recall or rehire.

Needless to say, you must be prepared to abide by the recall/ rehire policy you develop. A purely cosmetic policy is an open door to litigation.

Recall/rehire policies are anathema to some employers, who try to forbid reemployment of anyone who gets laid off. That's not a good idea, for such a policy is unfair and could easily be misconstrued.

Work force reductions and plant closings are scary for everyone involved. With sensible policies, though, you should be able to weather at least the legal storms by protecting your rights and those of the employees you must lay off. Just remember these things:

Give workers plenty of advance notice of a layoff or plant closing.

Don't let employee performance or other subjective factors affect your layoff decisions.

CHAPTER 9

IT'S IN THE CONTRACT

Although the at-will doctrine is still the cornerstone of the American employer-employee relationship, it's become chipped and eroded. You can no longer hide behind the at-will doctrine in a termination case.

Small wonder that more and more companies are switching from at-will employment to contractual arrangements with their workers. Not long ago, people believed that a contract boxed them in. That was before the law and the courts turned around and boxed in the at-will doctrine. Now, at least a contract will let you know exactly where you stand with your employees.

Contracts between employers and employees are playing an increasingly important role in the U.S. workplace. But contractual employment harbors its share of legal quicksand, too: The amount of litigation involving broken employment contracts is skyrocketing.

In one recent case, a former employee filed a $36 million breach-of-contract suit against a Los Angeles–based defense manufacturer. The ex-employee claimed that the company used threats and lies to get its employees to sign employment contracts and agreements not to work for competitors. It also tried to finagle employees into cheating the Department of Defense. When the employees balked at being a part of this shell game, the company fired them—in clear violation of the employment contracts they'd signed. The former employee asked the court to give him damages for alleged fraud, breach of contract, wrongful dismissal, and emotional distress.

If you keep getting knocked off your feet by termination suits, you may decide that pure at-will employment is more hassle than it's worth and that contractual arrangements are the way to go, at least for some aspects of your business. You must be careful, however, not to cobble up employment contracts that are just as fuzzy or confining as a modern at-will employment arrangement can be.

CONSULTANT OR EMPLOYEE?

If all your employees sign contracts, does that mean they suddenly turn into free-lancers or independent contractors? Probably not. When the Internal Revenue Service audits an employer, it uses these criteria to distinguish independent contractors from employees:

1. Contractors aren't required to follow instructions to do their work.
2. Contractors rarely receive training to do a job.
3. Contractors can subcontract or hire others to do work for them.
4. Contractors can also hire, supervise, and pay assistants without intervention from their employers.
5. Contractors set their own work hours.
6. Contractors decide where the work is done.
7. Contractors don't see their employers every day.
8. Contractors control the sequence of tasks leading to completion of jobs.
9. Contractors do not have to submit progress reports to their employers.
10. Contractors receive a fee for a job, not for the time spent doing the job.
11. Contractors cannot be paid for an incomplete job.
12. Contractors pay their own expenses.
13. Contractors usually furnish their own tools.
14. Contractors have (or should have) enough time to do work for more than one employer, and can show that they make their services available to other employers.
15. Contractors have a substantial investment in their trade that lets them remain independent of employer facilities.

16. Contractors cannot be fired at-will as long as they produce the result specified in their contracts.

Suppose, by these criteria, that certain "employees" prove to be independent contractors after all. You might think that your termination worries are over, because everything is plainly spelled out in their contracts. Believe me, contract workers can sue you for wrongful discharge just as easily as at-will employees can.

Too many organizations think that they can get away with using boilerplate agreements when they hire consultants—the same contract with each new contractor's name typed in. Bad mistake! Not all independent contracting situations are alike, so you should be prepared to sit down with each contractor and hash out the details. Extended wrangling might not be necessary; a standard contract might be perfectly acceptable to both sides. However, it's much better for you and the consultant to resolve any differences before the job begins than for the consultant to sue you for breach of contract or something equally nasty after the job ends.

Avoiding litigation from contract employees starts with finding the right consultant for the job. You must screen your independent contractors as rigorously as you screen your at-will employees. Before you hire a contractor, learn as much as you can about his or her education, professional certification and affiliations, financial and technical resources, and support staff. Make sure the contractor has liability insurance. And always obtain references from his or her previous clients!

The contract, of course, is what counts when you're working with contract employees. Your agreements with independent consultants should contain these elements:

1. A description of the experience and resources required to do the job.
2. A description of the services that the consultant will perform.
3. The deadline by which these services must be performed.
4. A description of fees and charges, including the consultant's billing rate and schedule, a cost breakdown, and a statement about who is responsible for paying taxes.

5. A listing of the staff who will work on the project, with a proviso that the consultant will replace these workers only if you agree.
6. A statement about who owns the final product of the consultant's work. (Careful with this one, especially when you're working with software developers.)
7. A nondisclosure clause to prevent the consultant from divulging your company's valuable proprietary information to outsiders.
8. A statement that frees you from blame or liability if the consultant does something wrong.

AN EMPLOYMENT CONTRACT PRIMER

An employment contract, like any other agreement, must contain certain essentials if it's to stand up in court (see Table 9–1).

Putting the contract in a standard format is necessary so that both sides understand their duties and responsibilities to each other. A side benefit is that standard-format contracts reduce the risk of litigation.

In law, form is often more important than substance. Many employers have lost suits because their employment contracts didn't include some crucial clause. Three things that employers tend to overlook are (1) the jurisdiction for court proceedings, (2) a listing of financial incentives to reward employees for good performance or for complying with an agreement, and (3) protection against the ravages of mergers and acquisitions.

Define the Jurisdiction

Some employers have an impossibly sunny view of the employment relationship. They figure they'll never have to worry about employment-related lawsuits, so they don't bother to insert anything in their employment contracts about where and in which courts cases involving those contracts will be tried.

Defining the jurisdiction for trials that might never happen may seem silly. From your perspective, however, it makes sense to take control of jurisdictional issues from the beginning of the employment arrangement. You'll save a lot of money and cut

TABLE 9–1
Possible Employment Contract Provisions

Provision	Comments
Duration of contract	Specific period Renewal procedures and options
Duties	Position Job description and responsibilities Support and facilities
Outside activities	
Compensation	Salary Bonuses and supplemental compensation
Fringe benefits	Insurance Vacation Sick leave Tuition reimbursement Transportation and travel
Termination	Basis for termination Time limits Procedures Notice required Handling of benefits
Restrictive covenants	Protection of confidential and proprietary information Protection of clients Geographic area Time Duty of good faith and loyalty
Breach of contract	Effect Actions waiving breach
Choice of law	Jurisdiction for hearing disputes Attorney's fees
Arbitration	
Indemnity and Advance of Expenses	
Disability	
Assignability	

down on the amount of human resources staff time required to prepare for the case. When your company is based in New York, you certainly don't want a former employee to sue you in a Los Angeles court!

The jurisdictional clause should give both the state and forum for potential court proceedings. For instance, you might have a contract with an independent consultant stipulating that all disputes or lawsuits involving the agreement will be heard in the district court of Middlesex County, Massachusetts. Also, be sure to include a statement that neither you nor the employee objects to the jurisdiction named in the contract, and that neither side will try to contest or change it if there is a trial.

These days, the court system has become so bogged down that a growing number of companies are submitting their employer-employee disputes to professional arbitrators instead of going to trial. If this option appeals to you, your employment contracts should say that arbitration will be the forum for resolving problems and that hearings will follow the rules of the American Arbitration Association.

Describe Financial Benefits

Companies often give incentives such as money or stock to employees for doing a good job—or for agreeing to resign on request. Whether you're hiring or firing, such incentives are bound to come up. Protect yourself by ensuring that your employment contracts outline the financial benefits that employees will receive, particularly if they belong to middle or upper management. No matter what kind of incentive you offer, describe it in the contract!

Popular financial incentives include:

Stock Options. The Internal Revenue Service considers some types of stock options taxable income. With incentive stock options employees get a tax break, but they don't receive any income if they exercise their option to sell the stock.

Stock Grants. Under a phantom stock plan, the amount of cash or stock paid to an employee depends on the value of the your company's stock. For example, the employee might receive cash equal to the appreciation in value of your company's stock at the end of a 10-year incentive period. The employee pays taxes on this payment; you can deduct it.

Under a restricted stock plan, you issue stock to the employee that isn't transferable and has a substantial risk of forfeiture—in other words, the employee loses the stock unless he or she meets certain conditions. You might, for instance, impose a restriction that if the employee leaves the company before the end of a five-year period, he or she will forfeit interest in the stock and will have to return it to the company.

Performance-Based Incentives. Some organizations pay cash bonuses to employees every year, often at Christmas. The amount of such a bonus depends on the organization's annual performance. Thus, employees might receive an annual bonus of 15 percent after a year in which the company thrives and 10 percent the following year when the company takes a loss.

You can set up a wide variety of incentive plans based on short- or long-term company performance. In a *performance share plan,* you award employees a specified number of shares of the company's stock at the beginning of an incentive period. If the employees meet your incentive goals, they actually receive the shares or a cash payment equal to the value of the stock. In a *performance unit plan,* you grant selected employees a targeted number of "performance units." If the employees meet their goals, they receive a specified dollar amount for each performance unit.

Deferred Compensation. You might decide to set up an *unfunded deferred compensation plan* so that managers or other high-paid employees can be exempt from the requirements of the Employee Retirement Income Security Act of 1974. The deferred benefits come from your company's general assets, making the employees general creditors of the company.

The structure of such plans ensures that employees have no income from the deferred compensation until they actually receive the money. You can usually take an income tax deduction when you pay out deferred compensation.

Open the Golden Parachute

Companies that eat up other companies often don't care about the employees they leave in their wake. The managers of the new, megalithic company may fire long-time employees or sweep away valuable benefits such as stock options.

When your company appears to be the target of a merger or acquisition, you can easily save jobs and benefits by including a special "golden parachute" clause in your employment contracts. Usually, such protection applies only to upper-tier managers, but you might want to extend it to other workers. The major drawback of golden parachute agreements is that employees may have to pay a hefty excise tax if the value of their protected benefits exceeds a certain amount.

SETTLING UP

Some employers like to have at least their top-level executives sign agreements that cover every nook and cranny of the employment relationship. Far more employers use contracts only to take care of potentially messy employment situations, such as tying up loose ends with terminated employees or preventing employees who leave the company from working for the competition.

Termination or settlement agreements are a way of releasing employers from work-related liability when they fire employees. Basically, the employer gives the terminated employee something he or she wants to keep him or her from suing for wrongful discharge, discrimination, or whatever.

Ask a terminated employee to sign a settlement agreement if you believe that the circumstances of the firing might lead to a lawsuit, if the employee has already made claims against your company and you don't have the documentation and witnesses to fight them, and if your company routinely obtains releases from all departing employees. Tread cautiously, however, if you think that requesting a release will make the employee suspect that the company has broken a law or will give the employee evidence of your discriminatory motives.

In some instances, a signed letter of resignation may be enough to fend off a lawsuit, so you won't need to bother with a settlement agreement.

Cover the Bases

Although settlement agreements may seem to provide the ultimate protection against termination suits, they can put you in a bit of a bind. You want the agreement to cover every possible contingency, even if that means the resulting document ends up looking like Groucho's endless contract in *A Night at the Opera*. But you don't want the employee to claim that you used fraud or coercion to get him or her to sign it. Unfortunately, the longer a contract is and the more legalese it contains, the less likely that an employee will sign it voluntarily. What can you do to avoid this trap?

The best course is to hammer everything out with the employee when he or she is terminated. Then, and only then, should you go ahead and draft the settlement agreement—in plain English, not legal gobbledygook.

Here, not in any particular order, are the basic elements of a typical settlement agreement:

1. A brief summary of the facts of the agreement, including those of its negotiation.
2. A brief description of the reasons for the agreement—for instance, to sever the employment relationship and resolve existing or potential disputes arising from it, or to sever the employment relationship with "no fault" liability for either side.
3. The effective date of the termination or settlement.
4. A listing of "consideration" (something of value given or done to make a binding contract) bestowed on the employee for signing the release, such as severance pay (which terminated employees usually don't get), compensation for unused vacation time, a letter of reference, or release from an agreement not to work for competitive firms.
5. A description of how benefits due the employee (unused vacation time, bonuses and other incentives, stock options, insurance coverage, and so on) will be handled.
6. A description of how the employee's unpaid loans and credit card balances will be handled.

7. A description of how savings plans will be handled. (You should tackle this issue even if the distribution of funds will strictly follow the the rules of the savings plan.)
8. A statement that the employee has not been coerced or enticed into signing the agreement, and that he or she is entering into the agreement freely because of the money or other consideration that he or she is receiving.
9. A statement that the employee has been advised of his or her right to seek legal advice, and has had a chance to discuss the agreement with an attorney of his or her choice.
10. A statement that neither you nor the employee will make disparaging remarks about one another, and that the employee won't discredit your company's services or products.
11. An acknowledgment that the employee has read the agreement and understands it.

To ensure that the employee really understands what the release involves, give him or her a specified period to mull over whether to sign it. If you wish, you can also specify a period during which the employee can cancel the agreement. Just remember to put both of these periods in the agreement.

You might want to think about including a confidentiality provision, which lets you and the employee tell the world that both of you have reached an agreement and are pleased with it—no need, in other words, for confidentiality. Another nice-to-have is a "no admissions" clause stating that both you and the employee deny violating each other's rights or breaking any contracts or laws.

Released!

You're probably wondering, "What about the good part—the release that frees me from pesky employee lawsuits?"

To make it all happen, you must get the employee to sign a covenant (formal agreement) that he or she will not sue your organization, file charges with government agencies, or join others in suing or filing charges stemming from claims against your organization. (After all, such claims should vanish as soon as the employee signs the settlement agreement.) If the employee has already initiated a suit, it's perfectly OK for you to ask him or her to drop it, as long as the court or agency goes along with the idea.

Make sure that the release protects your right to countersue the employee if he or she violates the covenant by suing or filing charges. Also, don't forget to state whether the employee must pay attorney's fees or damages if you win. For attorney's fees, stipulate that the employee should pay your attorney directly; the IRS might view a fee payment check made out to you as taxable income, even if the money is going straight into your attorney's pocket.

Workers' compensation claims are a major exception to such covenants. If the employee has a pending claim, note in the release that you have allocated a specific sum for the claim, to be paid on final approval of the settlement. You should also include a provision absolving both you and the employee from blame for breaches of the agreement caused by others.

The release should apply to all past, present, and future employment-related claims the employee may have against the company. To make the release truly airtight, extend it to cover the employee's heirs, executors, and "assigns" (people to whom he or she transfers property).

NO COMPETITION

Eric E. is on the verge of getting fired, but he beats you to the punch by quitting and immediately going to work for Tronitron, your company's biggest competitor. Within a few months, Tronitron comes out with a new product that looks suspiciously like your company's top-secret widget, which you'd been planning to unveil at the upcoming Widgetcon trade show. You know, of course, that Eric has passed along the widget design to Tronitron. You wonder sadly, "Could we have done anything to stop him?"

When employees leave your organization, there's no guarantee that they won't run off to work for the competition. It doesn't matter whether they get fired or leave under their own steam.

Legally, it doesn't even matter that your company suffers when another firm "steals" an employee.

Luckily, there's a way out: *noncompete agreements*. A non-compete agreement specifically prevents employees from working for competing organizations within a certain geographic area for a set period. Thus, you can breathe a little easier about the likelihood of your company's priceless trade secrets and inside information walking out the door with a departing employee.

Now for the bad news: Noncompete agreements are a legal gray area. Many judges don't like them at all. If your noncompete agreement ever comes under fire, you can bet that the judge will scrutinize it carefully to make sure that it does not represent an unreasonable restraint of trade.

By its nature, a noncompete agreement restrains trade. The key word is *reasonable*. To assess how reasonable your agreement is, the judge will try to determine whether the restraint of trade it entails is necessary to protect your business interests, and whether the agreement's objectives are legitimate and thus worthy of protection.

The courts have upheld noncompete agreements that applied to these workers:

1. Sales representatives who had personal contact with their employer's customers.
2. A company comptroller who had access to sensitive financial data and other trade secrets.
3. A limited partner of an insurance company who had access to confidential business practices and other trade secrets.
4. A manager who had access to confidential records, including a client list, pricing policies, and building techniques.
5. A company secretary/treasurer who had inside information that would have harmed a former employer.

Space and Time Limits

In assessing whether a noncompete agreement passes the reasonability test, judges take a hard look at its geographic restrictions and time limits, as well as the type of activity it forbids.

The main concern about geographic limits is whether they're too restrictive. The courts are likely to frown on an agreement that essentially bans an employee from every location where he or she might end up working for a competitor.

A lot depends on the kind of worker you're dealing with. You can, for instance, ask a member of your board of directors not to work for a competitive firm anywhere in the United States for a certain period. But you won't get away with putting a similar nationwide restriction on a nuclear power plant engineer.

In general, be conservative about geographic limits. A noncompete agreement that keeps an employee from working for a competitor within a 50-mile radius of your organization will probably pass muster.

Many employers get into trouble by setting ridiculous time constraints in noncompete agreements. There's no magic number of months or years; limits are largely situational. Thus, a three-year limit on a person who sells medical equipment is reasonable, as is a seven-limit on a partner in an insurance firm. But a five-year limit on a retail clerk is too long.

Where's the Competition?

Another sore spot is whether the job an employee wants to take represents a true competitive threat to your organization.

Let's say your company makes IBM® personal computer clones. You can restrict an employee from working for another PC clone manufacturer in the same geographic area. You may have a hard time making the noncompete agreement stick, however, if the competitive clone manufacturer hires your ex-employee to work in its video games division.

Again, restrictions on the scope of competitive activity cannot be too sweeping. An industrial supplies firm cannot prevent employees from getting involved with a similar business. Yet it's OK for the same firm to restrict a former employee from making contracts with its customers, even if the contracts are for items that the firm doesn't sell.

To be considered reasonable, a noncompete agreement cannot be harsh: It cannot bar an employee from practicing the vocation for which he or she is trained. Thus, if a former employee is a certified electrician, you can't stop him or her from getting a job as an electrician at another company within commuting distance of your firm.

As is true of just about everything in employment law, a noncompete agreement cannot offend public policy. Is the service the employee provides so important that attempting to restrict it would jeopardize the public good? Don't bother with a noncompete agreement if the answer is yes.

The courts draw the line at ambiguous agreements that don't describe exactly what kind of activity is prohibited. The rationale is that going along with such an agreement might also be going against public policy. And no court will rewrite an unenforceable agreement to make it enforceable.

Legal and Binding

One thing to remember about noncompete agreements and other formal employment contracts: You have to give the employee something (consideration) to make the agreement binding. The consideration can be anything from cash to job leads at noncompetitive firms.

Something else to remember is that the validity of the agreement ultimately depends on the law of the state where it is made. You can clarify matters immensely by inserting the governing law in the agreement itself—for instance, "This contract will be governed by the laws of Colorado."

What if an employee pulls a fast one by taking a job with a competitor after signing a noncompete agreement? You can, of course, go to court and ask for an injunction directing the employee to stop violating the agreement. Or you can ask the employee to pay damages to reimburse you for lost profits, which include certain overhead costs as well as profits in the usual sense. If the employee can prove that you didn't hold up your end of the bargain, however, the courts won't do anything for you.

BROKEN CONTRACTS

The down side of employment contracts is that it's not always easy to get people to live up to them. It doesn't matter whether you make all-encompassing contracts with consultants or employees, or just have employees sign noncompete or settlement agreements. Sooner or later an employee is going to leave you at the altar.

The employee may breach the agreement intentionally or because he or she doesn't know any better. That doesn't matter, either; ignorance is never an excuse under the law.

When employees do break their employment agreements, you have several legal options.

Interference with Business

You may be able to charge contract-breaking employees with "tortious interference" with your company's business. In law-speak, a tort is a wrongful act, injury, or damage not involving breach of contract. What you're doing here is showing that the employee has hurt your present and future business; breach of contract is a separate issue altogether.

A former employee can interfere with business by:

1. Using violence, intimidation, bribery, or fraud.
2. Abusing the employer's trust.
3. Filing frivolous or unfounded lawsuits.
4. Defaming the employer.
5. Violating an established standard of a trade or profession, say, by practicing "sharp dealing" and behaving unethically.
6. Enticing other employees of the former employer to leave.

If the employee has inveigled other employees into joining him or her in a competitive business venture, you can also claim interference with employment contracts.

To make a tortious interference charge stick, you must show that:

1. A valid contractual relationship or expectation of doing business existed.
2. The employee knew about the relationship or expectation.
3. The employee intentionally interfered with the relationship or expectation by doing something to terminate it.

4. Terminating the relationship or expectation hurt your business.

Conspiracy to Injure Business

Disgruntled former employees, particularly those who've been fired, sometimes get together to plan acts of sabotage against their former employee. Their goal is to damage the former employer's reputation and business, perhaps by starting up their own company whose sole purpose is running the former employer into the ground.

If you can prove that a former employee and at least one other person have maliciously and intentionally tried to harm your company, you can probably get them on charges of *conspiracy to injure business*. Proving conspiracy, however, can be tough.

You must demonstrate that the former employee's primary and overriding purpose was to hurt you. When the "injury" is simply a by-product of employees trying to get ahead in their own business, there's no conspiracy.

Also, conspiracy requires at least two people working together. Under the law, a former employee who goes to work for an unincorporated firm has no defense against conspiracy charges. An employee who goes to work for a corporation has built-in conspiracy protection, however, because the law states that corporations can't be found guilty of conspiring with their "agents" (employees).

Unfair Competition

Martha L. is leaving Sprockets Public Relations to become a free-lance promotional writer. While she's still at Sprockets, she tells a Dingbats Unlimited product manager with whom she's worked in the past that she's leaving the company. The Dingbats rep says, "That's too bad; we liked what you did for us." Martha, sensing an opportunity, says, "We don't have to stop working together! I'm starting a promo business, and I'd be happy to keep writing your press releases for you." As soon as Sprockets hears about Martha moving in on the Dingbats rep, it sues her for *unfair competition.*

Martha didn't goof when she solicited the Dingbats rep for business—that, after all, is what free enterprise is about. Her error lay in not waiting until she'd actually left Sprockets. Because she jumped the gun, she harmed Sprockets by taking business away from the company.

Until the employment relationship is severed, your employees must put your company's interests ahead of their own. They must be candid with you, and they shouldn't withhold information that might help you protect and promote your interests.

Once an employee leaves, he or she still owes something to you. But that doesn't necessarily mean a hands-off policy toward your customers. It's OK for an employee to solicit business from people he or she has worked with, as Martha did, as long as it's not explicitly forbidden by a noncompete agreement or other contract.

Misuse of Confidential Information

All employees have a legal obligation to maintain the confidentiality of trade secrets and other sensitive information they run across in their jobs. This is part of the employee's duty to show the utmost good faith, loyalty, and honesty toward his or her employer. Thus, an employee can't divulge corporate financial data, marketing strategies, or pricing policies to others.

The same principles of responsibility, fidelity, and honesty apply to former employees. An ex-employee who leaks, say, confidential bidding information to a competitor has violated a trust, and you can nail him or her for it.

To determine whether the information disclosed by a former employee actually qualifies as confidential, the courts look at several factors:

1. The extent to which the information is already known, both inside and outside the former employer's business. If it's common currency in the industry or can be obtained from trade publications, directories, and the like, it's not confidential.

2. Whether the information has been widely or casually available inside the former employer's company. If anyone from a mail clerk to a vice president can gain access to it, it's not confidential.
3. Whether the former employer has adequately guarded the information and told employees that the company considers it confidential.
4. The commercial value of the information to a competitor of the former employer. The information must be innovative or unique (something other than a compilation of nonsecret data) and must provide a demonstrable economic advantage to the competitor.
5. The amount of time and money the former employer spent to develop the information.
6. Whether the competitor or new employer could easily duplicate the information without the employee's help.
7. Whether the employee had a confidential relationship with the former employer.

There's no doubt that employment contracts can be a legal quagmire. Therefore, you must question whether a contract is really appropriate for your employment situation. Will it really cut down on lawsuits? What else will it buy you? Would you be better off with an at-will relationship?

If you do decide to go with contracts for any aspect of your employment relationship, keep these things in mind:

Work out the details before you draft the contract.
Make sure the contract contains all the right stuff, and put it in clear language.
Don't ever force an employee to sign a contract.

CHAPTER 10

—

THE PAPER CHASE

Paperwork, like death and taxes, is one of life's grim certainties. In your career, you have probably filled out reams of triplicate forms to order new supplies, move office furniture, and change light bulbs. So you'll probably groan deeply when I tell you that paperwork is a critical part of termination law.

Making your way through the labyrinthine maze of federal and state employment regulations demands more paperwork, and time, than ever. Letting the paperwork slide, however, can be extremely hazardous to your organization's health. Keeping good personnel records is necessary, of course, if you want to comply with the law—but it's also your best line of defense in employment-related lawsuits.

Poor recordkeeping can cost your company a bundle of money, as the following cases illustrate:

• A California real estate agency spent $250,000 to settle a federal racial discrimination case out of court. A black agent charged that the agency had denied her opportunities to earn commissions and other income that were available to white agents. She claimed that the agency shunted white customers to white agents and discouraged black agents from selling properties in white neighborhoods.

Unable to produce documentation showing that it didn't condone such business practices, the agency was up the creek in court. Even the firm's own lawyers said that "the company's concern with sales outweighed the recordkeeping requirements demanded of it by federal and state law."

• For five years, a Hispanic employee of an Ohio-based beer wholesaler watched as his white co-workers received special on-the-job training. His requests to participate in the training program regularly ended up in the circular file. Meanwhile, the man's supervisors noted in his performance evaluations that he did not seem to understand his job. Because his performance reviews were less than wonderful, he got smaller raises than did his white counterparts.

When the employee struck back with a discrimination suit, the company could not defend itself because it had kept such slipshod records of its training and promotion practices. The jury awarded the employee $3 million in punitive damages—one of the biggest judgments ever given to a victim of job discrimination.

• An aerospace manufacturer in Texas agreed to pay $7.5 million to 1,000 women who, according to the Department of Labor, had been "steered into traditionally female jobs" when they'd been hired. A compliance review found that the company had failed to follow Department of Labor regulations and various federal laws.

In litigation to determine whether an employer has acted appropriately in disciplining or firing an employee, cases are literally won or lost on paper. The courts usually aren't too sympathetic to companies with haphazard recordkeeping systems. In fact, the U.S. Supreme Court has held that an employer who can't produce proper business records has no right to complain about a judgment against him or her.

Every time you discipline or fire employees, you *must* leave a paper trail to document why you did what you did. You'll be hard pressed to defend a firing for poor performance, for instance, if the fired employee's personnel file is full of glowing job evaluations. And you'll be at the mercy of an employee's arbitrary treatment complaint if your records show that other employees have indeed been treated differently in the same situation.

WHAT DOES THE LAW WANT?

Bureaucracies love rules, and our federal and state governments are no exception. The array of statutes and regulations with which you must comply is amazing—and intimidating.

Your first impulse may be to ignore all this seemingly needless red tape and hope that you don't get caught. What you should ignore is that impulse! You must follow *all* the regulations scrupulously. Going along with government regulations not only puts you on the right side of the regulators, it also provides that critical proof of compliance you need to defend your organization in a wrongful discharge suit.

Not all the information I'm asking you to keep track of applies directly to firing or discipline. Nonetheless, it's the kind of information that you should be keeping on file as a matter of course—it's what the law asks for.

Wage Records

Various laws demand that you keep detailed records of your pay practices for all employees. You must maintain the following basic information for all workers, including those subject to the minimum wage provisions of the Fair Labor Standards Act (FLSA):

1. Name and address.
2. Date of birth (only for employees under 19 years of age).
3. Sex.
4. Occupation.
5. Time and day of the week when the employee's workweek begins.
6. The hourly wage rate for any week in which the employee works overtime.
7. The number of hours an employee works during each workday.
8. Total earnings due the employee for the hours that he or she has worked during a workday or workweek, including overtime.
9. Additions to or deductions from the employee's wages for each pay period.

10. Total wages paid to the employee in each pay period.
11. Dates of payments and the pay periods they cover.

You'll need exactly the same information for administrative and professional employees, executives, and outside salespeople. In addition, you must keep records of such employees' *total* remuneration for each pay period, including fringe benefits and perks.

Equal Pay Records

The Federal Equal Pay Act requires you to keep records that may determine whether discrepancies in pay are based on factors other than sex. These are the records that you should be keeping anyway:

1. Records concerning payment of wages.
2. Wage rates.
3. Job evaluations.
4. Job descriptions.
5. Descriptions of merit and seniority systems.
6. Collective bargaining agreements.
7. Descriptions of pay practices.

Hang on to these records, as well as anything else that might explain pay differentials for male and female workers, for two years.

THE OLD AND THE YOUNG

The graying of the Baby Boom generation has generated more and more age-related employment lawsuits. As we've seen, a fair number of termination cases involve older workers who claim that they've been unjustly put out to pasture. Rock-solid records are your only defense against charges of ageism.

Age Records

The Age Discrimination in Employment Act (ADEA) requires you to record each employee's name, address, date of birth, occupation, rate of pay, and weekly compensation. You must maintain these records for three years. You must also keep records on age-related employee benefit programs, such as pension and insurance plans, for the full period that each plan is in effect and for at least one year after its termination.

Any time you lay off, fire, or refuse to hire, promote, demote, transfer, or select an individual for training, make sure the information gets into your personnel files. You never know whether someone will claim that he or she was laid off or fired or demoted because of age. Hold on to these records for at least a year after the personnel actions to which they refer.

Needless to say, you shouldn't throw away descriptions of your seniority and merit raise systems. Even an outdated document may come in handy in court, if only to show the mutations that your policy has undergone.

Age Certificates

You may not think of yourself as an exploiter of child labor. If you hire your cousin's 15-year-old daughter for the summer without obtaining the right documentation, however, you might find yourself bumping up against the FLSA's child labor provisions.

To avoid running afoul of the FLSA, you must have a valid certificate of age on file for each employee under the minimum working age. These certificates, issued by the Federal Wage and Hour Division or a state agency appointed by the Secretary of Labor, are especially important when you're dealing with minors who claim to be only a year or two older than the minimum working age, or with workers who actually look younger than the minimum age.

Make sure that the age certificate for each minor contains this information:

1. The minor's name and address.
2. Place and date of the minor's birth, with a statement giving the source of this information (birth certificate, passport, parent's word).
3. The minor's sex.
4. The minor's occupation.
5. The minor's signature.
6. Name and address of the minor's parent or guardian.

7. Employer's name and address.
8. Nature of the employer's business.
9. Signature of the official issuing the certificate.
10. Date and place the certificate is issued.

If you fire a worker for whom you've obtained an age certificate, you must return the certificate to the official who issued it. The official can then use the document as proof of age for any subsequent certificates issued for the minor.

Employers who participate in special work-experience and career exploration programs approved by a state educational agency and the Federal Wage and Hour Division must also keep training agreements on file. The teacher or coordinator of the program, the employer, each student, and the student's parent or guardian must all sign the agreement, which must remain on file for the duration of the program.

FAIR IS FAIR

Employees often have trouble proving employer discrimination unless the employer really blows it. With good documentation to show that you treat your employees equitably, you may be able to knock an employee's discrimination charges right out of the ballpark.

EEOC Records

If your business employs 100 or more workers, you must report the racial and ethnic composition of your work force to the Equal Employment Opportunity Commission (EEOC). The EEOC allows you to survey your employees for the information, or to obtain it from postemployment records.

The EEOC requires this information as part of the Civil Rights Act of 1964, which, as you know, forbids discrimination based on race, religion, or national origin. But the commission adds an important caveat: It recommends that you keep records of race and ethnic heritage separate from personnel records.

That's because mingling the two sets of records might be considered evidence of discrimination.

The commission has its own rules for the retention of records on hiring, firing, promotion, demotion, transfer, layoffs, pay scales, and selection for training or apprenticeship. For example, it requires you to keep for six months the personnel records of an employee who has been fired. Likewise, if an employee files charges against you or if the EEOC initiates an action against you under Title VII, you must preserve all relevant personnel records until the matter is resolved. This includes employment records for the employee who believes that he or she has been discriminated against, as well as for all other employees holding similar jobs.

Hiring the Handicapped

Under certain conditions, you can pay disabled workers less than the minimum wage—for instance, if you run a sheltered workshop. If you wish to do so, however, you must apply to the Wage and Hour Administration for certification.

After the certificate has been granted and the disabled person hired, you must hang on to the certificate for at least three years. What's more, you must keep the personnel information for your disabled workers separate from those for other employees and precede the disabled workers' names with a symbol or letter that indicates their status.

OCCUPATIONAL HAZARDS

What do you do when a union is itching to sue you for hampering collective bargaining efforts, or when the government starts sniffing around your plant for alleged health and safety violations? Simple—you show them that you've filed the right forms and maintained the right records.

Labor Records

The Labor Management Reporting and Disclosure Act of 1959 requires you to file a report for any fiscal year in which:

1. You make a payment or loan to a labor organization or its officers, agents, or members.
2. You make a payment to union members so that they can alter the way other employees exercise their rights to organize and bargain collectively.
3. You spend money to interfere with employees' rights to organize and bargain collectively, or to restrain them from exercising these rights.
4. You spend money to obtain information about the activities of union members and other employees in connection with a labor dispute in which you are involved.
5. You make an agreement with a labor relations consultant or independent contractor, who acts on your behalf to affect the way employees exercise their rights to organize and bargain collectively.
6. You make an agreement with a labor relations consultant or independent contractor to supply you with information about the activities of union members and other employees in connection with a labor dispute in which you are involved.

In addition, you must maintain records that substantiate these reports for at least five years after they've been filed.

Health and Safety Records

The Occupational Safety and Health Act (OSHA) of 1990 requires you to keep a log of all occupational injuries and illnesses. You must note each injury or illness in the log no later than six working days after it happens. The agency that administers OSHA (also known as OSHA) provides its own log forms.

OSHA also requires supplementary records on each occupational injury or illness. The reports required for workers' compensation insurance are acceptable for this purpose.

Using OSHA-supplied forms, you must compile an annual summary of occupational injuries and illnesses. You need to complete the summary no later than one month after the end of each calendar year, and you must certify its truthfulness and completeness. Then you must post a copy of the summary in a place where your employees can easily see it, and mail copies to employees who don't regularly come in to your place of business.

Keep all your OSHA records for five years after the end of the year to which they refer. If you have employees who are covered by the Longshoremen's and Harbor Workers' Compensation Act, you must also retain records concerning injuries that affect them.

THE TAX MAN COMETH

Rules, regulations, and records are the lifeblood of the Internal Revenue Service. If you've ever had the extremely unpleasant experience of being audited, you know that good records can save your hide—and that bad or nonexistent ones can send you up the river.

Employers who withhold income tax from employees' wages must keep explicit tax records. The two most important types of records pertain to Social Security and unemployment taxes.

If you must pay tax under the Federal Insurance Contributions Act (FICA), you must also keep a record of all compensation paid to your employees. You must do the same thing for tax paid under the Federal Unemployment Tax Act (FUTA).

FUTA also requires you to maintain records of:

1. The total amount of compensation (cash or otherwise) paid to each employee during the calendar year, including any amount withheld for tax or other reasons.
2. The amount of wages subject to taxation under FUTA.
3. The amount of contributions paid into a state unemployment fund.

WORKING WITH UNCLE SAM

The federal government gives a lot, but it asks a lot in return. In exchange for doing business with it, for instance, it extracts promises from its contractors that they'll comply with a mountain of government-mandated workplace policies.

Contractors, be forewarned: The Department of Labor takes these policies *very* seriously. The records must be on hand and readily available to the department to use in evaluating your compliance. The government considers noncompliance to be a breach of contract, which could result in your losing the contract and even being blackballed from future contract consideration.

Most government agency contracts contain stipulations about wage rates, overtime, use of child labor, job safety, and the like. If these stipulations apply to you, you must maintain the following information for at least three years after the date of the last entry:

1. Name, address, sex, and occupation of each employee covered by the contract.
2. Date of birth of each employee under 19 years of age.
3. Payroll records for each employee, including wage rates and amounts paid during each pay period, the hours worked each day and each week, and the period during which each employee worked on the contract.

With few exceptions, government contractors and subcontractors must comply with equal employment opportunity regulations that require documentation of hiring and promotion practices. Contractors may also have to file copies of their affirmative action plans and provide annual options.

RECORDKEEPING HINTS

Maintaining personnel records is much like performing a high-wire balancing act over a busy intersection. Act precisely and attentively, and you're home free. Make one false move, and you're dead.

Obviously, skimpy personnel files leave a company open to lawsuits. But so do thick files crammed with information that the courts consider irrelevant and perhaps discriminatory.

Just as you shouldn't hire an employee without obtaining the right job application form, résumé, and recommendations, you shouldn't discipline or fire an employee without providing documentation to explain the need for such drastic action. This is the kind of personnel file information that effectively backs up a firing:

1. Detailed observations by the employee's supervisors.
2. Notes about pertinent incidents and rule infractions leading up to the termination.
3. Work samples, if relevant.
4. An explanation of the necessary qualifications for the job.

What you want to do is make sure that your company's personnel records work for it, not against it.

A good place to begin is with *semiannual updates*. Check the files a couple of times a year to ensure that their contents are accurate and that no major gaps exist. Along with fixing mistakes, you should eliminate extraneous and potentially damaging information.

As a rule of thumb, the personnel documents that you develop and maintain should be *genuinely useful*. All too often, a company is accused of discrimination because its files contain meaningless, irrelevant data that has no real impact on termination or any other aspect of employment. It's sound business practice to assess periodically whether your company really needs the information that it asks for in its personnel forms.

Become familiar with personnel documents so that you can avoid surprises. You'll be in a better position to evaluate employee claims against you if you know what's in the files. Moreover, systematically maintained personnel files are a great asset in court cases that compare a wide range of employees.

Squeaky-Clean Files

The linchpin of a useful records system is a process that regularly gets rid of information that the law no longer demands. The trick is to keep the data you need without inadvertently removing anything. Don't throw the baby out with the bath water!

For example, employees' home addresses must be on file during their entire tenure with your company. Even though a job application is often the source of an employee's address, however, you can safely discard job applications after one year. Filing home addresses separately lets you remove the job application from an employee's file after the appropriate time has elapsed.

In addition to weeding out documents that you're no longer legally obligated to hang on to, you should eliminate outdated and irrelevant personnel documents, such as old performance reviews. Keep enough of these older documents around, however, to defend your company against possible lawsuits. You might amend your automatic one-year-dump policy for job applications and résumés, for instance, so that you can have enough documentation to establish an employee's qualifications for being hired.

Records, records, records! Sometimes it may seem as if you're drowning in a sea of paperwork. Never forget, though, that the records you fill out today may be your savior tomorrow. And keep this in mind:

Clear and accurate records can make the difference between a firing that appears justified and one that seems arbitrary and unfair.

CHAPTER 11

21ST-CENTURY TERMINATION

The only sure thing about forecasting the future is that there are no sure things. Nonetheless, it is possible to look at what's going on now and conjecture likely directions and trends; in fact, the most accurate visions of the future are usually just extensions of the present. So, examining what's happening in the American workplace now can give us a pretty good idea of what termination law might be like beyond the year 2000.

Not long ago, futurists predicted that demographic changes would completely alter the American work force by the turn of this century. But the Hudson Institute found that only a handful of employers are currently developing programs to deal with these changes. That means an awful lot of organizations are going to get caught short by increasing government regulations, an overloaded court system, and a flood tide of employment-related litigation over the next decade.

Some employers think they'll stay off the hook if they put all their stock in the venerable at-will rule. Basically, however, at-will employment is a dying duck. Federal and state laws tell you not only who you can fire or lay off, but also how, when, and why. You can bet that there will be more, not fewer, laws as we round the corner to the 21st century. And more laws will mean more lawsuits.

Admittedly, this is not a pretty picture. The outlook for your 21st-century workplace doesn't have to be so bleak, however, if you start preparing *now*. Gauging which way the legal winds are blowing should give you a good idea of what termination law will be like in the next decade.

ON THE DISCRIMINATION FRONT

Discrimination, real or otherwise, lies at the heart of many termination suits. Employees who wish to charge their former employers with discriminatory firings or layoffs have an unprecedented amount of legal ammunition at their disposal, from Title VII of the Civil Rights Act of 1964 to the Americans with Disabilities Act of 1990 to the Age Discrimination in Employment Act (ADEA). But many workers, and their elected representatives, believe that this arsenal needs even more firepower.

As of this writing, Congress is considering legislation that would bring about fundamental changes in the nation's civil rights laws. Advocates who want to strengthen state laws against job discrimination are pressing for similar bills in their state legislatures.

Civil rights advocacy groups say that Title VII of the landmark 1964 Civil Rights Act is a sound law, but it just doesn't go far enough. If Congress passed the legislation that these groups are clamoring for, employees would be able to take their employment discrimination cases directly to a jury instead of having to deal with the Equal Employment Opportunity Commission (EEOC) first.

Think settlements and damages paid to ex-employees are out of sight now? If Congress expands Title VII to give winning employees the right to ask for compensatory and punitive damages, million-dollar awards may become the norm in 21st-century employment discrimination cases.

Conservative members of Congress want to keep Title VII the way it is, but they appear to be outgunned. There are strong indications that an expanded civil rights act will eventually make it through both houses.

A stronger civil rights agenda is, of course, a good thing. What you want to watch out for is employees who try to use it to clobber you for lapses in your firing and layoff policies. Using the suggestions in this book, you should be able to develop termination procedures that can stand up to the toughest civil rights legislation.

Minority Women and the Ladder

You'll probably hear a lot more from women of color in your 21st-century workplace.

Female workers who are members of minority groups start the employment game with two strikes against them, as far as the reigning Old Boy network is concerned. White women complain about the so-called glass ceiling that keeps them out of the highest corporate echelons. But women of color, who must contend with both racism and sexism, haven't even been able to breach the middle-management ranks.

African-American women represent just 2 percent of the managers in companies with 100 or more employees, according to the EEOC. Three percent of these managers are black men, and 23 percent are white women. There still are no black women on *Black Enterprise* magazine's roster of the top 25 black managers in corporate America.

This situation is bound to change, especially as more black women enter the job market. By the year 2000, there may be more than 8 million African-American women in the U.S. work force. It's a good bet that these women will do whatever is necessary to get the courts and legislatures to guarantee them equal access to all the rungs on the corporate ladder.

Government watchdogs will doubtless force employers to promote deserving minority women to management positions in the future. The regulators have already told companies that they can't lay off workers of color first just because they were hired last. And they've nailed companies to the wall for using specious reasons to fire or lay off talented black workers who would otherwise have been on the inside track for management jobs. With more stringent laws behind them, the regulators should be just as aggressive about pursuing employment justice for black women.

I've already told you the best way to avoid the aggravation of having female minority employees sue you for discriminatory firings or layoffs: Treat such workers exactly the same as you treat all other workers. If you must fire a black female employee, have a legitimate reason, give her enough warning and plenty of chances to improve her performance or change her behavior, and work out a termination agreement before she gets any ideas about going to court. Likewise, ensure that layoffs don't seem to zero in on female employees of color.

Light versus Dark

Regrettably, racism remains the scourge of the American workplace. But white employers aren't the only ones who may be guilty of judging employees by their skin color rather than their job performance.

African-American skin tones run the gamut from bluish-black to pale ivory. Since slavery days, whites and even some African-Americans have favored light-skinned blacks. Not surprisingly, dark-skinned blacks have come to resent those with lighter skin.

Recently, for instance, a light-skinned African-American worker claimed that her dark-skinned supervisor had fired her because of his skin color prejudices. She testified that the supervisor gave her darker co-workers better job assignments and made snide remarks about how she "needed some sun" and had had life too easy.

The federal judge who heard this case ruled that the employee did not offer enough evidence to demonstrate that she was fired because of the supervisor hated light-skinned blacks. The case was, nonetheless, a landmark decision—the first time in the United States that one black person had filed a civil discrimination suit against another. Several similar cases are pending in the courts.

If you or your managers are people of color, be careful! This area may become a source of legal fireworks in the near future. Remember: Whether you're white, black, or green, skin color has no place in the termination process.

Heavyweight Hassles

Are you among the millions of Americans fighting the Battle of the Bulge? If you're male, your co-workers may rib you about your weight gain; most likely, it will be a private matter between you and your fitness club. If you're female, however, extra pounds might cost you your job.

Several major U.S. airlines have fairly strict weight requirements for their flight attendants. Until recently, such standards applied only to female attendants. Men were allowed to become "robust" with age; women who did not maintain slim, girlish figures were summarily dismissed.

The airlines have learned a partial lesson: They now have weight requirements that supposedly apply to both men and women. In general, though, women have been the ones fired for "excess baggage."

But that may change in the next few years. The EEOC has filed a class-action lawsuit against one of the biggest airlines in the United States for firing female flight attendants who don't meet its weight standards. The EEOC's suit contends that the airline's weight policy, which states that a 5'5" female attendant cannot weigh more than 129 pounds, discriminates against attendants over the age of 40. It's also rough on attendants who gain weight while taking a leave of absence to have a baby or to work for their union, because the airline doesn't give them any time to slim down before they go back on the job. (Some attendants have speculated that the weight restrictions may be a sneaky way of getting rid of union activists.)

An attorney for the airline has said that the weight policy is not discriminatory because it applies to both male and female flight attendants. The airline allegedly bases its policy on an insurance company chart that assigns maximum body weight by height, with more weight allowed for men.

Whether the airline or the fired flight attendants win, employees' weight is going to remain an issue for as long as the culture thinks slim is beautiful. Just keep in mind that you cannot fire overweight female workers merely because clients like slender women. (Men, as usual, seem not to enter into this debate.) If you do impose weight limits for health or safety reasons, make sure you enforce them for both sexes.

More Clout for the Aging

Some termination trends are easier to spot than others. For instance, I think we can be fairly certain that older workers will file more and more job discrimination suits under the ADEA in the coming years.

Even though the U.S. population is aging en masse, too many employers still think that young workers are somehow inherently better than older ones. They claim that a seasoned veteran's years of experience are no match for the up-to-date training of a young hotshot just out of school. (Also, some employers reason that they can get away with paying the young hotshot less.)

Many older people feel that the ADEA doesn't do enough to protect older Americans against ageism in employment. Advocates are aiming for tougher sanctions against employers who use age as an excuse to fire or lay off workers. To bolster the ADEA, Congress and the state legislatures will probably target retirement programs and employees' waivers of their rights under the act.

You, and your work force, aren't getting any younger. Now is the time to evaluate your organization's procedures and policies for anything that might smack of age discrimination. Take a particularly hard look at your retirement and seniority programs.

Rights for the Disabled

The Rehabilitation Act of 1973 protects disabled employees from discrimination in hiring, promotion, and termination if—and that's a big if—they work for the federal government or its contractors. Until summer 1990, disabled workers had no real shield against job discrimination by companies in the private sector.

Count on sweeping changes, however, once the courts begin to enforce the Americans with Disabilities Act of 1990. This act makes it illegal for private-sector employers to discriminate against disabled workers in hiring, firing, discipline, promotion, and all other aspects of employment. And, despite loud objections by conservative legislators, the act's protection extends to workers with AIDS.

The importance of the Americans with Disabilities Act goes far beyond the disabled employees it protects: It also serves as a model for state disabled-rights bills. We should see plenty of action in this arena in the years ahead.

The upshot is that you should no longer consider your company litigation-proof if it fires or lays off a disabled worker, or if it declines to make "reasonable accommodations" for disabled workers who are otherwise qualified for employment.

The Telltale Gene

Law often has a hard time keeping up with technology. Although employers can now ask their employees to undergo genetic screening to reveal hereditary tendencies toward certain conditions, existing laws offer no answers to the troubling questions raised by such tests.

The glitch here is that not every person with a genetic predisposition toward a disease automatically develops that disease. Even if you carry the gene for alcoholism, you're not irretrievably fated to become an alcoholic. We're the products of both heredity and environment; some genes don't express themselves unless environmental conditions are exactly right. Of course, this hasn't stopped employers from using genetic tendencies as benchmarks for hiring and firing.

Labor unions and civil liberties advocates worry that medical science may be about to create a new underclass of high-risk employees. Mounting pressure on employers to reduce health care costs could lead to genetic discrimination against job applicants or employees with a higher-than-usual risk of illness or disability.

Medical screening is not new; in fact, employers started requiring preemployment physicals as early as 1910. Not until the past few years, however, have employers tried to zero in on employees who are *likely to develop* a disease or disability, rather than those who *actually have* a medical problem.

At present, Congress is trying to figure out whether existing social protection schemes and pension systems can ensure the economic security of high-risk workers. It's also looking at legislation to protect high-risk workers against discrimination.

The Employee Retirement Income Security Act already forbids employers from firing or otherwise discriminating against employees at high risk for disease. The Americans with Disabilities Act of 1990 and the Rehabilitation Act of 1973 may also give high-risk employees a legal umbrella against job discrimination.

As genetic testing becomes more common, however, there will be a great deal of pressure on Congress and the state legislatures to pass legislation aimed specifically at protecting high-risk workers. At the forefront of this movement is New Jersey, with its statute preventing employers from firing, refusing to hire, or discriminating against workers because of "any atypical hereditary cellular or blood trait."

CHILD CARE AND FAMILY LEAVE

Most organizations now have some kind of maternity leave policy. Usually, such policies give a female employee a certain number of weeks off to have her baby, along with an assurance that her job, or a similar position, will be waiting for her when she goes back to work. Women who stay out longer than the allotted six or eight weeks may forfeit their jobs.

It's taken corporate America a long time to get to this point. Some states still have no statute that mandates a maternity leave period and guarantees job security for pregnant employees. For the most part, however, maternity leave is not as much of a hot potato as it used to be.

Many professional women, heeding the ticking of their biological clocks, are putting their careers on hold temporarily to have babies. Unfortunately, the usual eight-week maternity leave is seldom long enough to handle the demands of caring for a very young infant—and it doesn't apply to househusbands who take time off to be with their new children. So, the rich farm their infants out to expensive nannies or child care facilities. The poor leave their babies with unlicensed daycare providers or relatives.

Working women are trying to get Congress to do something about child care. One proposed solution is for companies to provide in-house daycare; legislative efforts are afoot to give tax benefits to employers who offer child care assistance to their employees. Another idea is a mandatory period of unpaid family leave.

Recently, a family and medical leave bill made it through both houses of Congress but was vetoed by the president, who claimed that it would cost American businesses too much. If the bill had become law, it would have required both public- and private-sector employers to give workers up to 12 weeks of unpaid medical leave to care for a new baby, an adopted or sick child, or a seriously ill spouse or elderly parent. Workers could also use the 12 weeks to obtain treatment for their own medical problems.

The legislation would not have applied to businesses with fewer than 50 workers, or to the highest-paid workers. But affected employers would still have had to continue health insurance for employees on leave. Moreover, companies would have had to give returning employees their old jobs back or find them equivalent positions.

Although the first federal family leave bill bombed out, a modified version may sail past both Congress and the executive branch within the decade. Once it does, expect the states to pass their own mandatory family and medical leave statutes.

In some ways, a mandatory leave policy will make it easier for you. You won't have to fire employees who stay at home with their babies when their maternity leave gives out, or who take a lot of time off to have an operation or care for an ailing parent. But you will have to make sure that your leave policies are in tune with the law, whatever that turns out to be. Definitely stay on top of this issue!

SAFE AND HEALTHY WORKPLACES

Asbestos in the light fixtures. Diseases circulating through the ventilation system. Carpets that emit toxic fumes. The modern office can indeed be hazardous to workers' health—and that assessment doesn't even begin to take into account the problems caused by human error or negligence.

Although Congress recently gave the Occupational Safety and Health Act (OSHA) more teeth, it believes that civil penalties aren't enough to teach corporate violators a lesson. Congress wants to impose tougher criminal sanctions on employers who intentionally violate the act. That means supervisors might be subject to both civil and criminal penalties—even if they didn't actually know anything about the OSHA violations.

The implications for your termination policy are clear: If you keep a "hazardous" worker, such as an unregenerate drug user, on staff in a position where he or she can harm other others, you may face jail as well as a stiff fine. Firing employees who refuse to work under conditions that violate OSHA regulations may also earn you a prison sentence if Congress toughens the act.

No Smoking at Work

Those dire warnings on cigarette packs and billboards seem to be working. Fewer Americans are smoking than ever before. Moreover, the nonsmoking majority is vociferously telling the smoking minority where to take its coffin nails—out of the workplace.

Evidence indicates that secondhand cigarette smoke is extremely dangerous to nonsmokers. That's why more and more companies are restricting employee smoking to certain parts of their facilities when they're not banning it outright.

The city councillors of Takoma Park, Maryland, had originally intended to come up with a law that mirrored other workplace smoking regulations. Currently, the laws of many jurisdictions prohibit smoking in work areas shared by at least three employees, but permit smoking in private, enclosed offices or in designated smoking areas. The city councillors apparently felt that limiting smoking was no answer to the secondhand smoke problem, however, so they went all the way and approved one of the nation's toughest smoke-free workplace laws.

"Smokers have every right to kill themselves, but they can't kill others," said the bill's sponsor. "Our intention is to protect the health and safety of the public."

Takoma Park may be just one tiny town, but it's not alone in its aversion to the evil weed. Several dozen states and municipalities now regulate smoking in the workplace. Growing concern with the health of workers will surely prompt greater regulation in the future.

Your company may have joined the vanguard of the antismoking drive by establishing a smoke-free office. Because a smoking ban is a company rule, you're within your rights if you terminate employees who keep lighting up at work. As more cities and states pass mandatory workplace smoking bans, firing employees who defy antismoking regulations should become even less of a legal liability.

Video Hazards

Your best data entry operator is pregnant. "I can't spend eight hours or more in front of my terminal," she says, "because it might hurt the baby." "Balderdash!" you reply. "You're just malingering. If you don't want to pull your shift like everyone else, there's the door." The operator sues you for wrongful discharge.

No, it hasn't happened yet, but it might. The Environmental Protection Agency has already documented the potential threat of video display terminals (VDTs) to the health of the people who use them, especially for extended periods. At some progressive companies, employees who spend most or all of every workday at their VDTs are reimbursed for eye care. Other organizations are developing policies on pregnant employees and VDT use. (This one's hard to call because the scientists haven't given us the last word yet on whether VDT emissions are harmful to fetuses.)

Several cities and states have begun to regulate the working conditions of VDT operators, but the federal government has yet to take action. As electronic offices proliferate and the white-collar work force expands, however, there will be more efforts to regulate the use of terminals. VDTs have also become a hot topic with labor unions, so I doubt that the issue will disappear from the congressional agenda any time soon.

Stressed-Out Employees

One workplace hazard that probably hasn't crossed your mind is stress. Big deal, you say. It's impossible to work or, for that matter, live in the modern world without stress. The courts, however, are starting to disagree. When an unusually stressful work situation causes an employee to crack, he or she may well be eligible for workers' compensation. Whether you or anyone else perceives the situation as stressful is irrelevant.

For example, a woman who had worked for a federal contractor in Massachusetts for 22 years had a nervous breakdown when the company told her that she was going to be transferred to another department. A Massachusetts state court ruled that she was entitled to workers' comp because her breakdown was a "personal injury arising out of and in the course of . . . employment."

In another, rather peculiar case, a white sanitation supervisor for the city of Louisville, Kentucky, made out like a burglar when he blamed his severe depression on the stress of having to work with blacks. Along with awarding the man maximum benefits, the Kentucky Workers' Compensation Board ordered the city to give him a job in which he would work only with whites.

In the eyes of some, job stress is as much of an occupational illness as black lung. Its victims include workers who can't do their jobs because they're worried about being laid off, and those who drink too much because they can't handle new responsibilities. If such employees live in a state that pays workers' comp benefits to job stress victims, they may be able to collect almost all of their pay while staying home!

The workplace isn't going to be any less stressful in the 21st century. There will be new technology to deal with, new demands on workers. Count on federal and and state legislation that grants employees even more leeway in making job stress claims.

THE PRIVACY RIGHTS GAMBLE

Before you terminate an employee, you need to know something about his or her work performance and on-the-job behavior.

There are many ways to obtain this vital information, some legitimate and some shady. The future may be a bit more complicated, though: Information-gathering techniques that are perfectly legal now may bump up against increasingly stringent regulations to protect employee privacy in the years ahead.

Watching Big Brother

Using video or electronic surveillance may seem like a terrific way to keep tabs on employees. When the monitoring system catches Jane making endless personal long-distance calls or

John stealing company property, you have irrefutable proof of wrongdoing and can take appropriate disciplinary action. Also, a surveillance program that, say, lets you know periodically what employees are doing at their computers boosts security and gives you insights into employee performance and productivity.

Employees, of course, do not believe that surveillance systems are the greatest thing since the radial tire. For instance, the Communications Workers of America, one of the most powerful unions in the country, has been lobbying Congress to outlaw abuses of employee surveillance. The legislation they're pushing for appears to take aim at employers who electronically monitor work performance and production standards. But the bill's scope is so broad that it would effectively eliminate the use of video and other surveillance techniques as well.

Congress seems to be moving in the direction of protecting employee privacy rights at the expense of employers' rights under the at-will doctrine. Thus, it's not out of the question that the Communication Workers' proposed legislation, which has been knocking around the halls of Congress for years, might become law some time in the next decade.

Drug Testing and Privacy

Few aspects of modern employment law are more contorted than drug testing. Employers need to know whether employees are ingesting substances that might hamper their productivity and possibly endanger others. But employees claim that drug testing is intrusive and offensive, a clear violation of their sacrosanct privacy guarantees.

Will we be able to unravel the drug testing mess by the 21st century? Probably not.

Congress and the state legislatures have recognized the necessity of drug testing—there are simply too many workers on drugs. But that hasn't deterred advocates from pushing federal and state legislation that would regulate the way in which employers test their employees.

In the coming years, the Department of Labor and its sister state agencies are sure to play a greater role in regulating the drug testing process. Current laws governing federal contractors already give the department a voice in this area.

The work environment is changing rapidly. By the year 2000, many of your employees are likely to be women and members of minority groups, so you'll have to be constantly on guard for employment practices that seem discriminatory. You'll also have to pay more attention to employees' health and safety needs. And, you'll have to live with even more government regulations than you do now, impossible as that may seem.

Dealing with termination in this brave new work world is going to be ticklish. By following the guidelines I've given you in this book, however, you should be able to steer clear of employee lawsuits and EEOC complaints. If you implement sound termination policies and stay on top of changes in the employment laws, your layoffs and firings will almost always be smooth exits!

INDEX